A SHORT COURSE IN SPOKEN ENGLISH

Ronald Mackin

A SHORT COURSE IN SPOKEN ENGLISH

ENGLISH LANGUAGE SERVICES
in association with
OXFORD UNIVERSITY PRESS, LONDON & NEW YORK

ENGLISH LANGUAGE SERVICES
A Division of Washington Educational Research Associates, Inc.
14350 Northwest Science Park Drive
Portland, Oregon 97229

Oxford University Press, Ely House, London W1
GLASGOW NEW YORK TORONTO MELBOURNE
WELLINGTON CAPE TOWN IBADAN NAIROBI DAR ES SALAAM
LUSAKA ADDIS ABABA DELHI BOMBAY CALCUTTA
MADRAS KARACHI LAHORE DACCA KUALA LUMPUR
SINGAPORE HONG KONG TOKYO

ISBN 0-87789-137-0 English Language Services
ISBN 0-19-453062-0 Oxford University Press
© Oxford University Press, 1967
United States edition © Oxford University Press 1975

This course was originally published by Oxford University Press,
London, under the title: A COURSE IN SPOKEN ENGLISH;
TEXTS, DRILLS AND TESTS.

Illustrated by Dennis Mallet

United States edition first published 1975

Printed in the United States of America

Acknowledgments

As the author of the original course on which *A Short Course in Spoken English* is based, I should like to express my thanks to all those who have been concerned in the production of this adapted version for learners who are more interested in American than in British English.

Marcia Evans has faithfully preserved those elements of the course which have, I am told, commended it to other users — in particular the *grading*, which is based primarily on the complexities of the English verb; the *variety* of situations; and the interplay of personalities in family scenes. She has not only retained, but has improved on what was hopefully a certain light-heartedness in approach. It is indeed a skilful and sensitive adaptation.

Dennis Mallet has provided a new set of drawings for this edition. His illustrations are apt, clear, helpful and often very funny, as one would expect of a man who for longer than I dare mention has been a well known contributor to *Punch*.

I am grateful to John Dermody whose special knowledge of the teaching situations in which this course is most likely to be used is apparent in the *Introduction for the Teacher*. I am sure that many teachers will be grateful to him for the advice that he offers.

The admirably recorded texts and drills were made under the expert direction of Peter Bartlett. American voices are used throughout.

I cannot omit mention of the careful reading of the manuscript by David Sawer (of Oxford University Press); and still less of my gratitude to Dick Evans for undertaking and directing the whole project.

RONALD MACKIN
September 1974

A word for the teacher

A Short Course in Spoken English is intended for those who have already studied English at school or elsewhere but without achieving any real mastery of the spoken language. From the point of view of material and structure, it is particularly suitable for refresher and repeat courses, and for advanced courses of unequal student composition at adult schools, language schools and similar educational institutions. It is also suitable:
  a) for students with a basic knowledge who wish to improve their language proficiency;
  b) as supplementary material to textbooks where insufficient emphasis has been placed on communications skills;
  c) for schools using language labs and seeking extra material as a useful supplement to the set texts.

In some countries, the course has been used as the central part of the curriculum over a complete academic year; in other countries it is used in highly concentrated courses of as little as three weeks. It has been found useful in a remarkable range of situations, including the upgrading of teachers who have never taught English before and who may be required quickly in large numbers when English is introduced at a lower age-level in schools.

THE COURSE AT A GLANCE

Each of the ten units contains three kinds of material:
1. *Texts:* language used in meaningful contexts.
2. *Drills:* particular structural points exercised so that their use becomes automatic, though often with some requirement of selection on the part of the learner.
3. *Written Exercises:* review exercises for reinforcement.
   Tapes: Tapes are available to accompany the *Texts* and *Drills.*

IN DETAIL

The *Texts* are written with two primary objectives in mind: to present, in a reasonably progressive manner, the main features of the Verb (Phrase), and to do so in a variety of situations which permit the use of contrasting styles of the spoken language. The Table of Contents in the book clearly shows the development of these two themes by stating first the title of each text, which is an indication of the situation and to some extent of the degree of formality and informality of the style in which it is written, and then the main grammatical point which is being dealt with.

Each *Text* introduces several occurrences of a particular feature of the verb, *but in such a way that the learner's interest is focused on the subject matter, the situation and the style, rather than on the grammar.*

Text A is usually presented in equal sections, each containing groups of single utterances. Unlike many approaches of the past, however, these utterances are sequenced meaningfully to provide maximum retention on the learner's part. In addition, an oral reproduction exercise using the pictures will be easier to perform because of the sequencing.

Text B is written in dialogue form. Supplemented with pictures, the dialogues provide a basis for dramatizations, guided conversations and insights to colloquial usage and cultural values. The dialogues are so written that the recordings rarely run more than two minutes. Each dialogue is repeated three times, as follows:

(a) *The first run-through:* The student simply listens to the conversation.

(b) *The second run-through:* The student repeats the words of *one* of the speakers. Ample pauses are left on the tape to give him time to do this comfortably.

(c) *The third run-through:* This time the student takes the part of the character whose words he repeated during the second run-through. In this way he is gradually drawn into a fully participatory role. If he cannot recall the words of the character he is replacing, he can either refer to the book or, preferably, work through the recorded version a second time — or as many times as are necessary. The great advantage of working with recorded material, of course, is that the "model" is always the same; whereas when the teacher repeats a text he rarely does so without making some changes, whether in articulation or intonation.

DRILLS

When the student has worked through a *Text* in the manner described, his attention is then directed strictly to the grammatical patterns by means of the *Drills.* In addition to problems associated with the verb, the course deals with numerous other grammatical points and questions of usage which invariably prove difficult for the learner: the use of the indefinite article in sentences like "He is a doctor" and the absence of a corresponding form in "They are doctors"; the use of *this, that* and *it* in sentences like "Is this/that John?" "No, it's Peter"; the use of *how much* and *how many*; the comparative and superlative forms of adjectives; counting; the writing and speaking of dates, telling (the) time; the position of adverbs, and so on.

These *Drills* are varied, and range from the simple "Listen and repeat" type to those which require some selection on the part of the learner. In such cases the desired response is indicated by means of introductory examples, in which a second voice teaches the student how to respond to the first speaker. Drill B in Unit 7, for example, begins as follows:

Unit 7, Drill B. Listen
1. Teacher: Will he arrive at 11 o'clock?
   Stimulus: (No/at 10 o'clock)
   Student: No, he won't. He'll arrive at 10 o'clock.
   Teacher: No, he won't. He'll arrive at 10 o'clock.
   Student: No, he won't. He'll arrive at 10 o'clock.
2. Teacher: Will you be on the platform?
   Stimulus: (No/in the audience)
   Student: No, I won't. I'll be in the audience.
   Teacher: No, I won't. I'll be in the audience.
   Student: No, I won't. I'll be in the audience.
               Now you do the same.

This is then repeated, with pauses instead of the Student's Voice. The sequence is therefore:

1. Teacher's Voice (and stimulus)   2. Student's Response
3. Model   4. Student's Repetition

The introductory examples of each *Drill* are given in the book, but for the remainder on tape he must rely on his ear. Thus in Unit 7, Drill B, he has to go through four sequences in addition to those which are printed in the book; the only additional assistance he is given is the short list of new words that occur in them. The total number of sequences is given in parentheses at the head of each *Drill*.

WRITTEN EXERCISES

The *Written Exercises* are all arranged in workbook style, so that the answers can be conveniently written in the book. Whenever possible, they should be gone over orally first; the student should then write down the answers in pencil, so that if he makes a mistake it can be altered. He will then eventually compile his own "key", which will be useful for purposes of review.

The *Written Exercises* are numerous and varied in kind. Many are of a transformational nature: others are of the blank-filling or multiple-choice type. Several require the construction of sentences from given elements, on the basis of a model. All are strictly related to, and based on, the material which is presented in the *Texts* and *Drills*.

TEACHING METHOD

The method of use will vary according to the standard already reached by the student, the number of students in the group, the number of hours available each day or each week, and the language laboratory time available.

The teacher's role in the use of these *Texts, Drills* and *Written Exercises* is just as important as in the more usual kind of teaching. The difference is that the tape-recording relieves him of the burden of acting as a more or less mechanical model.

The machine does the mechanical work; the teacher guides, checks and helps the student both in the classroom and in the laboratory, if one is available. In the absence of a laboratory, the value of a single machine with a good loudspeaker, operated by the teacher, should not be underestimated.

How the meaning of the texts, etc. should be taught is left to the teacher. If necessary, translation can be used provided it is made clear to the learner that "understanding of meaning" does not equate with "ability to use", but that on the contrary it is only the first stage in the process.

A NOTE ON THE VOCABULARY

The course is essentially intended to provide students with a fresh approach to English, with special attention to its spoken forms. Most of those who use it will not be beginners and may therefore be presumed to have some "recognition" knowledge of the language.

It is a well-known phenomenon in language-learning that students may take a "recognition" knowledge to be a "complete" knowledge, especially where vocabulary items are concerned. Faced with a review course in which the objective is the "productive" use of language, students are inclined to become impatient if they feel that they already "know" all the words. For this reason, the author has deliberately used many words which are probably new to the learner. The student's interest will be more readily retained if he is satisfied that he is not only achieving spoken mastery of the main structures of English, but is building up his vocabulary at the same time.

Contents

NOTE. The grammatical grading is based on the main difficulties associated with the verb in English. Many other points of grammar are dealt with in the Course, but in the following list of contents only the features of the verb, which are of central interest, are mentioned.

UNIT 1

Page

TEXT A *People* 1
The verb *be*, present tense, affirmative, interrogative, positive, negative. The simple present tense, affirmative, positive.
Drills A—I 3
TEXT B *Talking about People* 6
Interrogative forms with *Who, What, Where, How old.*
EXERCISES A—G 7

UNIT 2

TEXT A *Mr. and Mrs. Parker* 15
The simple present tense, continued: interrogative; negative.
Do as a substitute verb.
Drills A—D 17
TEXT B *Introducing the New Manager* 19
Drills E—F 23
EXERCISES A—F 24

UNIT 3

TEXT A *The Parker Family* 31
The verb *have* as a full verb, present tense.
Drills A—C 33
TEXT B *A Medical Examination for Life Insurance* 35
Drills D—E 38
EXERCISES A—E 39

UNIT 4

TEXT A *A Visit to the Parkers* 43
The simple past tense referring to past time, regular and irregular verbs, positive and negative.
Drills A—E 47
The simple past tense, interrogative forms.
TEXT B *On Vacation* 49
Drill F 51
EXERCISES A—E 53

UNIT 5

Page

TEXT A   *The News*   58

The present perfect tense, affirmative; positive and negative.

Drills A–C   59

The present perfect tense, interrogative.

TEXT B   *The Parkers at Breakfast*   61

Drills D–G   64

The verb *want* in the patterns: *want to do something* (D); *want somebody to do something* (E).

EXERCISES A–E   66

UNIT 6

TEXT A   *A Running Commentary on the Kentucky Derby*   71

The present progressive (or continuous) tense, referring to present time.

TEXT B   *A Conversation about the Kentucky Derby*   73

The past progressive tense.

TEXT C   *The Weekend*   74

The present progressive tense, referring to future time. *Going to . . .*

Drills A–D   77

EXERCISES A–E   79

UNIT 7

TEXT A   *Arrangements for the Visit of the Mayor of New York*   85

will in the formal announcement of future events, positive and negative.

Drills A–D   87

will, won't affirmative; positive and negative. Informal style. Question tags with *will* and *won't*. *'ll* with pronouns and nouns, referring to the future.

TEXT B   *The Boss Comes to Dinner*   89

'll, will, won't in conversation. *Shall* in offers of assistance: *Shall I* etc?

Drills E–I   92

The present perfect, negative, with *yet*; the present perfect, positive, with *already*. The pattern *tell somebody to stop doing something*. Orders with and without the pronoun *you*.

EXERCISES A–F   94

UNIT 8

TEXT A   *Anne's visit*   99

Various question-tags

Drills A–D   101

TEXT B   *Last-minute Instructions*   103

have to, used to indicate obligation. The present tense referring to future time in clauses beginning *if, when, as soon as, until* etc.

Drills E–G   106

EXERCISES A–E   107

UNIT 9

Page

TEXT A   *Animal, Vegetable or Mineral* (1)   114
The modal verbs *can, can't; could, couldn't* associated with conditional
clauses; *may* used to indicate (i) permission (ii) possibility; *might, would,
wouldn't.*

Drills A—C   118

TEXT B   *A Lazy Saturday Afternoon*   119
The modal verbs: *should, shouldn't; ought to; don't have to; must.* The
construction *Let's do something.*

EXERCISES A—C   121

UNIT 10

TEXT A   *An International Exhibition*   125
The passive voice in a formal announcement.

Drills A—B   126

TEXT B   *Talking About Income Tax*   127
The passive voice in conversation.

Drill C   128

TEXT C   *A Lovers' Quarrel*   130
The *-ing* form in more complicated verbal groups.

Drill D   133

EXERCISES A—C   134

xiii

Unit 1 □ *Text A*

PEOPLE

1. This is Miss Jones.
   She's American.
   She comes from New York.
   She works in a hospital.
   She's a nurse.
   She's twenty-three.

2. That's Mr. Gordon.
   He's Canadian.
   He comes from Toronto.
   He's a teacher.
   He teaches in a school.
   He's thirty-six.

3. This is Mr. Parker.
   He's American.
   He comes from New York.
   He works in a department store.
   He's an assistant manager.
   He's fifty-six.

4. This is Mrs. Parker.
   She's American too.
   She comes from Baltimore.
   She's a housewife.
   She's fifty-six.

1

6.   Those boys are English.
They come from London.
Their names are Dick and Paul.
Dick is eighteen and Paul is
    eighteen, too.
They're twins.
They're students.

5.   These girls are American.
They come from Boston.
Their names are Jane and Nancy.
Jane is nineteen and Nancy's
    twenty.
They're students.

7.   Is this Mr. Parker?
Yes, it is.
Is he American?
Yes, he is.

8.   Is that Mr. Parker?
No, it isn't. It's Mr. Gordon.
Is he American?
No, he isn't. He's Canadian.

Drills

T = Teacher   S = Student

DRILL A [1] *(10)*   □ *T: Unit 1, Drill A. Listen!* □

1.   T: This is Miss Jones.   S: This is Miss Jones.
      T: This is Miss Jones.   S: This is Miss Jones.
2.   T: *Miss Ross.*   S: This is Miss Ross.
      T: This is Miss Ross.   S: This is Miss Ross.
3.   T: *Miss Allen.*   S: This is Miss Allen.
      T: This is Miss Allen   S: This is Miss Allen.
          T: Now you do the same.
      [2] **New names in this drill:** Ross; Allen.

DRILL B *(5)*   □ *T: Unit 1, Drill B. Listen!* □

1.   T: Is this Dick? *Yes.*   S: Yes, it is.
      T: Yes, it is.   S: Yes, it is.
2.   T. Is that Dick? *No.*   S: No, it isn't.
      T: No, it isn't.   S: No, it isn't.
          T: Now you do the same.

DRILL C *(8)*   □ *T: Unit 1, Drill C. Listen!* □

1.   T: Is Mr. Parker American? *Yes.*   S: Yes, he is.
      T: Yes, he is.   S: Yes, he is.
2.   T: Is Miss Jones Canadian? *No.*   S: No, she isn't.
      T: No, she isn't.   S: No, she isn't.
3.   T: Is this man American? *Yes.*   S: Yes, he is.
      T: Yes, he is.   S: Yes, he is.
4.   T: Is that woman Canadian? *No.*   S: No, she isn't.
      T: No, she isn't.   S: No, she isn't.
          T: Now you do the same.
      [2] **New words:** man; woman

[1] The numbers in parentheses after Drill A, Drill B, etc. represent the number of questions asked or statements required on the tape recordings.
[2] New names and new words occur on the tape recording but do not appear in the text.

DRILL D *(10)*   □ *T: Unit 1, Drill D. Listen!* □

1. **T:** Mr. Parker comes from New York.   **S:** He comes from New York.
    T: He comes from New York.   **S:** He comes from New York.
2. **T:** Mrs. Gordon comes from Toronto.   **S:** She comes from Toronto.
    T: She comes from Toronto.   **S:** She comes from Toronto.
3. **T:** Jane and Nancy come from Boston.   **S:** They come from Boston.
    T: They come from Boston.   **S:** They come from Boston.
4. **T:** Dick and Paul come from London.   **S:** They come from London.
    T: They come from London.   **S:** They come from London.
        T: Now you do the same.

DRILL E *(5)*   □ *T: Unit 1, Drill E. Listen!* □

1. **T:** Is Miss Jones a nurse? *Yes.*   **S:** Yes, she is.
    T: Yes, she is.   **S:** Yes, she is.
2. **T:** Is Mrs. Parker a nurse?
        No/a housewife.   **S:** No, she isn't. She's a housewife.
    T: No she isn't. She's a housewife.   **S:** No, she isn't. She's a housewife.
        T: Now you do the same.

DRILL F *(10)*   □ *T: Unit 1, Drill F. Listen!* □

1. **T:** Are you a nurse? *Yes.*   **S:** Yes, I am.
    T: Yes, I am.   **S:** Yes, I am.
2. **T:** Are you a teacher? *No/a nurse.*   **S:** No, I'm not. I'm a nurse.
    T: No, I'm not. I'm a nurse.   **S:** No, I'm not, I'm a nurse.
        T: Now you do the same.
New words: doctor; receptionist; typist; bank teller; an engineer

DRILL G *(6)*   □ *T: Unit 1, Drill G: Listen!* □

1. **T:** My friend is a teacher.
        My friends.   **S:** My friends are teachers.
    T: My friends are teachers.   **S:** My friends are teachers.
2. **T:** Your friend is an engineer.
        Your friends.   **S:** Your friends are engineers.
    T: Your friends are engineers.   **S:** Your friends are engineers.
3. **T:** This woman is a receptionist.
        These women.   **S:** These women are receptionists.
    T: These women are receptionists.   **S:** These women are receptionists.
        T: Now you do the same.
New words: (a) plural forms of nouns already used
          (b) my, friend(s), receptionist(s), men, women.

DRILL H *(6)*   □ *T: Unit 1, Drill H. Listen!* □

1. **T:** Are your friends nurses? *Yes.*   **S:** Yes, they are.
    T: Yes, they are.   **S:** Yes, they are.
2. **T:** Are those girls American?
    No/English   **S:** No, they aren't. They're English.
    T: No, they aren't. They're English.   **S:** No, they aren't. They're English.
    T: Now you do the same.

Unit 1 □ *Text B*

TALKING ABOUT PEOPLE

1. Who's this?
    It's Mr. Cardinali.
    What nationality is he?
    He's Italian.
    Where does he come from?
    Rome.
    What's his job?
    He's a mechanic.
    How old is he?
    He's forty-one.

2. Who's this?
    It's Mr. Volkers.
    What nationality is he?
    He's Dutch.
    Where does he come from?
    Rotterdam.
    What's his job?
    He's a business executive.
    How old is he?
    He's forty-eight.

DRILL I *(15)*   □ *T: Unit 1, Drill I. Counting in English. Listen and repeat.* □

1. **T:** One, two, three, four, five.
2. **T:** Six, seven, eight, nine, ten.

6

ORAL AND WRITTEN EXERCISES

EXERCISE A

(a)   First Conversation   (b)   Second Conversation

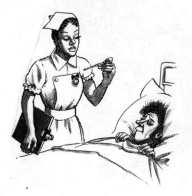

(a) First Conversation	(b) Second Conversation
1. . . . . this?	1. . . . . this?
2. . . . . Miss Jones.	2. . . . . Gordon.
3. What nationality . . . . ?	3. What nationality . . . . ?
4. . . . . American.	4. . . . . Canadian.
5. . . . . does . . . . come from?	5. . . . . does . . . . come from?
6. . . . . from New York?	6. . . . . from Toronto?
7. . . . . does . . . . work?	7. . . . . does . . . . work?
8. . . . . in a hospital.	8. . . . . in a school.
9. . . . . her job?	9. . . . . his job?
10. . . . . nurse.	10. . . . . teacher.
11. . . . . old is . . . . ?	11. . . . . old is . . . . ?
12. . . . . twenty-three.	12. . . . . thirty-six.

EXERCISE B   *Describe the people in these pictures.*

Example:

Mr. Owen / American / San Francisco / bank teller / 33

1. *This is Mr. Owen*
2. *He's American*
3. *He comes from San Francisco*
4. *He's a bank teller*
5. *He's thirty-three*

(a)

Mr. Strauss / American / Chicago / butcher / 38

1. ....

2. ....

3. ....

4. ....

5. ....

(b)

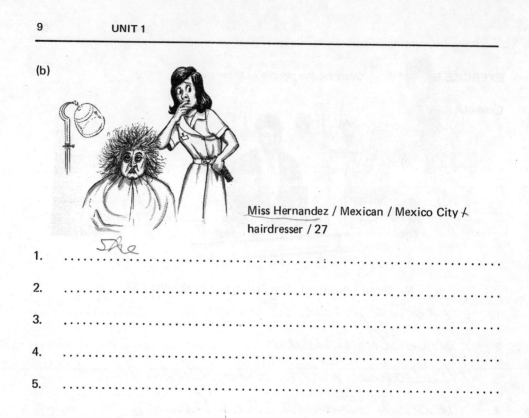

Miss Hernandez / Mexican / Mexico City /
hairdresser / 27

1. She ....

2. ....

3. ....

4. ....

5. ....

(c)

Mrs. Fox / American / Detroit / doctor / 42

1. ....

2. ....

3. ....

4. ....

5. ....

(d)

Miss Kugimoto / Japanese / Tokyo /
stewardess / 24

1. ....

2. ....

3. ....

4. ....

5. ....

(e)

Miss Ali / Iranian / Tehran /
radio announcer / 30

1. ....

2. ....

3. ....

4. ....

5. ....

EXERCISE C

Put the following sentences into the interrogative form.

Example: This is Mrs. Volkers.   *Is this Mrs. Volkers?*

1.   This is Miss Jones.   ....

2.   These girls are American.   *Are* ....

3.   These girls are Canadian.   ....

4.   That's Mrs. Parker.   ....

5.   She's American.   ....

6.   Those boys are Mexican.   ....

7.   They're students.   ....

8.   Dick and Paul are twins.   ....

9.   They're English.   ....

10.   Mrs. Parker's a housewife.   ....

11.   Miss Jones is a nurse.   ....

12.   She's twenty-three.   ....

13.   Those men are engineers.   ....

14.   These boys are twins.   ....

15.   Miss Ali's a radio announcer.   ....

EXERCISE D

Give the missing words:

1.   Is this Dick?   Yes, ...

2.   Is that Mrs. Parker?   No, ...

3.   Is Mr. Volkers a business executive?   Yes, ...

4.   Is Mr. Parker a business executive?   No, ...

5.   Is Miss Jones a nurse?   Yes, ...

6.   Is Paul a teacher?   No, ...

7.   Are you a student?   Yes, ...

8.   Are you a teacher?   No, ...

     . . . .

9.   Are you an engineer?   No, ...

     . . . .

10. Are you American?   No, ...

     . . . .

11. Is Mrs. Parker a receptionist?   No, ...

     . . . .

12. Is Jane a housewife?   No, ...

     . . . .

13. Is your friend a doctor?   No, he . . . .

     . . . .

14. Is your friend a nurse?   No, she . . . .

     . . . .

15. Is Mr. Parker Canadian?   No, ...

     . . . .

EXERCISE E

Put these sentences into the plural as in these examples:

This girl is American.	*These girls are American.*
That boy is a student.	*Those boys are students.*

1. This boy is Canadian. ....

2. That man is a doctor. ....

3. This woman is a teacher. ....

4. That nurse is my friend. ....

5. This student comes from London. ....

6. This girl works in New York. ....

7. That teacher comes from Toronto. ....

8. This radio announcer is Iranian. ....

9. This woman is a stewardess. ....

10. She's a hairdresser. ....

11. She's a doctor. ....

12. He's a bank teller. ....

13. He's a butcher. ....

14. He's an assistant manager. ....

15. He isn't a business executive. ....

EXERCISE F

Give the missing words:

1. Are these boys English?   Yes, ...

2. Are those girls English?   No, ...

3. Are Mr. and Mrs. Parker American?   Yes, ...

4. Are Mr. and Mrs. Gordon American?   No, ...

5. Are Jane and Nancy students?   Yes, ...

6. Are these men engineers?   Yes, ...

7. Are these women engineers?   No, ...

                                           . . . .   nurses.

8. Are your friends business executives? Yes, ...

9. Are these students Irish?   No, ...

                                           . . . .

10. Are Mr. and Mrs. Volkers Canadian?   No, ...

                                           . . . .

EXERCISE G

Say these numbers and write them in words:

1 . . . .   3 . . . .   6 . . . .   5 . . . .   8 . . . .

7 . . . .   4 . . . .   9 . . . .   10 . . . .   13 . . . .

15 . . . .   12 . . . .   14 . . . .   18 . . . .   20 . . . .

16 . . . .   19 . . . .   21 . . . .   26 . . . .

30 . . . .   50 . . . .   70 . . . .   43 . . . .

91 . . . .   85 . . . .   100 . . . .   101 . . . .

Unit 2 □ *Text A*

MR. AND MRS. PARKER

PART ONE

Mr. and Mrs. Parker live in Elmhurst.
They don't live in the center of New York.
Elmhurst is a suburb of New York.

Mr. Parker works in a department store.
He doesn't work at home.

Mrs. Parker stays at home.
She doesn't go out to work.

Mr. Parker goes to work five days a week.
He doesn't go to work *every* day.
He stays at home on Saturdays and Sundays.

PART TWO

Mr. and Mrs. Parker live in a house.
They don't live in an apartment.
They own their house.
They don't rent it.
It has a back yard.
It doesn't have a front yard.

Mr. Parker owns a car.
He doesn't own a motorcycle.
He goes to work by train.
He doesn't go to work by car.

PART THREE

Mr. Parker earns a hundred and fifty dollars a week.
He spends about thirty dollars a week.
He buys a commuter ticket for the train.

He eats lunch in the store cafeteria.
He doesn't eat lunch at a restaurant.

He smokes cigarettes.
He doesn't smoke cigars.

Mrs. Parker spends about seventy-five dollars a week.
She pays all the bills.

Drills

DRILL A *(6)*   □ *T: Unit 2, Drill A. Listen!* □

1.   **T:** Mr. Parker smokes cigarettes. *Cigars.*   **S:** He doesn't smoke cigars.
   T: He doesn't smoke cigars.   **S:** He doesn't smoke cigars.
2.   **T:** Mr. and Mrs. Parker live in Elmhurst. *Boston.*
                       S: They don't live in Boston.
   T: They don't live in Boston.   **S:** They don't live in Boston.
     T: Now you do the same.

DRILL B *(8)*   □ *T: Unit 2, Drill B. Listen!* □

1.   **T:** Does Mr. Parker live in a house? *Yes.*   **S:** Yes, he does.
   T: Yes, he does.   **S:** Yes, he does.
2.   **T:** Do Mr. and Mrs. Parker live in the center of New York? *No.*
                       S: No, they don't.
   T: No, they don't.   **S:** No, they don't.
3.   **T:** Do they live in a suburb of New York? *Yes.*
                       S: Yes, they do.
   T: Yes, they do.   **S:** Yes, they do.
     T: Now you do the same.

DRILL C *(9)*   □ *T: Unit 2, Drill C. Listen!* □

1. T: Do you smoke cigars? *No.*   S: No, I don't.
    T: No, I don't.   S: No, I don't.
2. T: Do you smoke cigarettes? *Yes.*   S: Yes, I do.
    T: Yes, I do.   S: Yes, I do.
3. T: Do you smoke cigars? *No/cigarettes.* S: No, I don't. I smoke cigarettes.
    T: No, I don't. I smoke cigarettes.   S: No, I don't. I smoke cigarettes.
        T: Now you do the same.

DRILL D *(10)*   □ *T: Unit 2, Drill D. Listen!* □

1. T: Do Mr. and Mrs. Parker live in
        Elmhurst or in the center of
        New York?   S: They live in Elmhurst.
    T: They live in Elmhurst.   S: They live in Elmhurst.
2. T: Does Mr. Parker earn a hundred or
        a hundred and fifty dollars a
        week?   S: He earns a hundred and fifty dollars
                                                a week.
    T: He earns a hundred and fifty dollars
        a week.   S: He earns a hundred and fifty dollars
                                                a week.
3. T: Do you live in a house or in an
        apartment?   S: I live in an apartment.
    T: I live in an apartment.   S: I live in an apartment.
        T: Now you do the same.

Unit 2 □ Text B

INTRODUCING THE NEW MANAGER

PART ONE

Mr. Parker:	This is one of our Ladies' Wear Departments.
Mr. Hammer:	It's very attractive.
Mr. Parker:	Miss Drummond. Could you come here a moment please?
Miss Drummond:	Good morning, Mr. Parker.
Mr. Parker:	Good morning. This is Mr. Hammer.
Miss Drummond:	Our new manager?
Mr. Parker:	That's right.
Miss Drummond:	How do you do, Mr. Hammer.
Mr. Hammer:	How do you do, Miss Drummond.

"HOW DO YOU DO,
MR HAMMER"

"I SELL... SKIRTS, SLACKS, SWEATERS AND BLOUSES"

PART TWO

Mr. H:	What do you sell, Miss Drummond?
Miss D:	I sell sportswear — skirts, slacks, sweaters and blouses.
Mr. H:	Where do you keep the skirts?
Miss D:	On these racks.
Mr. H:	I see. Do you sell many long skirts?
Miss D:	Oh yes. They're very popular now.
Mr. H:	Even in summer?
Miss D:	Yes. These days women wear them all year round.
Mr. H:	What about pantsuits?
Miss D:	These synthetic ones are very popular.
Mr. H:	Fine. What do you keep in those drawers?
Miss D:	We keep sweaters in them.

PART THREE

Mr. H:	Do you sell many long-sleeved sweaters?
Miss D:	Yes, but not in the summer.
Mr. H:	I suppose you sell a lot of blouses in the summer?
Miss D:	Yes, we do.
Mr. H:	What kinds?
Miss D:	All kinds — cotton, nylon, silk, rayon . . . and mixtures of course.
Mr. H:	What kinds of cardigans do most women prefer?
Miss D:	The V-necked kind, I think.
Mr. H:	Especially in matching sets, I suppose?
Miss D:	Yes, that's right.
Mr. H:	When do you sell most matching sets?
Miss D:	In the winter.
Mr. H:	Thank you, Miss Drummond. Er . . . by the way . . .
Miss D:	Yes, sir?
Mr. H:	What's in this box?
Miss D:	My lunch.
Mr. H:	Oh, I see. Where do you eat your lunch?
Miss D:	I eat it in the park, if it's nice.
Mr. H:	And if it isn't?
Miss D:	In the staff room.

"MY LUNCH"

DRILL E *(8)*   □ *T: Unit 2, Drill E. Listen!* □

1.   T: Where does Mr. Parker live?   S: He lives in Elmhurst.
      T: He lives in Elmhurst.   S: He lives in Elmhurst.
2.   T: Where does Miss Drummond eat
         her lunch?   S: She eats it in the park.
      T: She eats it in the park.   S: She eats it in the park.
3.   T: Where do you come from? *Japan*   S: I come from Japan.
      T: I come from Japan.   S: I come from Japan.
         T: Now you do the same.

DRILL F *(8)*   □ *T: Unit 2, Drill F. Listen!* □

1.   T: What does Miss Drummond sell?
         Sportswear.   S: She sells sportswear.
      T: She sells sportswear.   S: She sells sportswear.
2.   T: What does Mr. Parker smoke?
         Cigarettes.   S: He smokes cigarettes.
      T: He smokes cigarettes.   S: He smokes cigarettes.
3.   T: What do you smoke?
         A pipe.   S: I smoke a pipe.
      T: I smoke a pipe.   S: I smoke a pipe.
         T: Now you do the same.

ORAL AND WRITTEN EXERCISES

EXERCISE A

Put these sentences into the negative.

Examples:

I smoke cigarettes.

I don't smoke cigarettes.

He smokes a pipe.

He doesn't smoke a pipe.

1. I come from New York.

. . . .

2. Paul comes from London.

. . . .

3. Mr. Parker goes to work on Saturdays.

. . . .

4. He works six days a week.

. . . .

5. Mr. and Mrs. Parker live in an apartment.

. . . .

6. They rent their house.

. . . .

7. Miss Drummond stays at home on Sundays.

. . . .

8. Mrs. Parker goes out to work.

. . . .

9. You own a motorcycle.

. . . .

10. You earn a hundred dollars a week.

. . . .

EXERCISE B

Put these sentences into the interrogative.

Example:
Miss Ali lives in Tehran.   *Does Miss Ali live in Tehran?*

1.   Mr. Parker owns a car.   . . . .

2.   He works five days a week.   . . . .

3.   He goes to work by train.   . . . .

4.   Mrs. Parker stays at home.   . . . .

5.   Mrs. Parker pays all the bills.   . . . .

6.   They live in a suburb of New York.   . . . .

7.   Nancy comes from Boston.   . . . .

8.   Mr. Gordon teaches in a school.   . . . .

9.   Miss Jones works in a hospital.   . . . .

10.   She smokes cigarettes.   . . . .

11.   She has lunch in the store cafeteria.   . . . .

12.   She rents her apartment.   . . . .

13.   Her friends come from Ireland.   . . . .

14.   They rent their apartment.   . . . .

15.   These students own a car.   . . . .

EXERCISE C

Answer these questions as in the examples:

(a)   Does your friend come from Argentina? (Yes)

Yes, he does. ....

(b)   Do you come from Argentina? (No/Brazil)

No, I don't. I come from Brazil. ....

1.   (a)   Do you work in a school? (Yes)   ....
     (b)   Does Miss Jones work in a school? (No/in a hospital)

....

2.   (a)   Does Miss Hernandez come from Mexico? (Yes)

....

     (b)   Do Mr. and Mrs. Volkers come from Mexico? (No/Holland)

....

3.   (a)   Do Dick and Paul come from London? (Yes)   ....
     (b)   Do Jane and Nancy come from London? (No/Boston)

....

4.   (a)   Do you live in an apartment? (Yes)   ....
     (b)   Do Mr. and Mrs. Parker live in an apartment? (No/in a house)

....

5.   (a)   Do you own a car? (Yes)   ....
     (b)   Does Paul own a car? (No/a motorcycle)

....

6.   (a)   Does Mrs. Parker go to New York by car? (Yes) ....
     (b)   Does Mr. Parker go to New York by car? (No/by train)

....

EXERCISE D

Write questions for these answers.

Examples:

(a) *Where does Miss Jones work?*
(Miss Jones) She works in a hospital.

(b) *Where do Mr. and Mrs. Parker live?*
(Mr. and Mrs. Parker) They live in Elmhurst.

Begin each question with the word *Where*

1. ....
(Miss Drummond) She eats it (her lunch) in the park.

2. ....
I come from Japan.

3. ....
(Dick and Paul) They come from London.

4. ....
(Miss Hernandez) She comes from Mexico City.

5. ....
(My friends) They live in an apartment.

6. ....
(These women) They live in Boston.

7. ....
(Mr. Volkers) He eats it (his lunch) in a restaurant.

8. ....
(Mr. Gordon) He teaches in a school.

9. ....
(Miss Ali) She's in Tehran.

10. ....
(The doctor) He's at home.

EXERCISE E

Give the missing words:

1. What's this? It's a . . . .

2. What's this? It's a . . . .

3. What's that? . . . . car.

4. What's that? . . . . blouse.

5. What's this? . . . . bill (or check).

6. . . . . ? . . . . pipe.

7. . . . . ? . . . .

8. . . . . ? . . . .

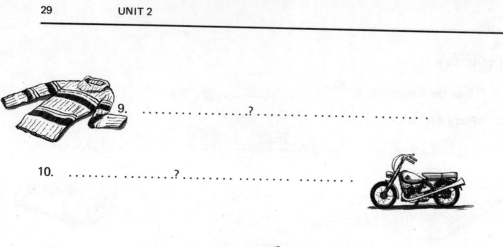

9. ? . . . .

10.   . . . . ? . . . .

11.   What are these? They're . . . .

12.   What are these? They're . . . .

13.   What are those? . . . . cars.

14.   . . . . ? . . . .

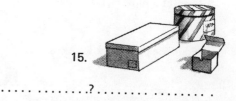

15.

. . . . ? . . . .

16.   . . . . ? . . . .

EXERCISE F

Write questions for these answers.

Examples:

(a) *What does Miss Drummond keep on those racks?*
(Miss Drummond) She keeps skirts on them. (those racks)

(b) *What does Mr. Parker smoke?*
(Mr. Parker) He smokes a pipe.

Begin each question with the word *What*.

1. . . . .
(Miss Drummond) She sells sportswear.

2. . . . .
(Mr. Parker) He smokes cigarettes.

3. . . . .
He owns a house and a car.

4. . . . .
He buys a commuter ticket for it. (the train)

5. . . . .
(Mrs. Parker) She pays all the bills.

6. . . . .
I sell sweaters, blouses, slacks and skirts.

7. . . . .
My lunch is in it. (that box)

8. . . . .
I smoke a pipe.

9. . . . .
(Paul) He owns a motorcycle.

10. . . . .
(This woman) She sells underwear.

Unit 3 □ *Text A*

THE PARKER FAMILY

PART ONE

Mr. and Mrs. Parker have five children.
They have three daughters and two sons.
They have three grandchildren.

Their daughters' names are Sylvia, Anne and Eileen.
Their sons' names are John and Bob.
Sylvia's their oldest daughter.
John's their older son.
Eileen's their youngest daughter.
Bob's their younger son.
Sylvia has two sisters.
She has two brothers.
The Parkers' youngest child is Eileen.

PART TWO

Anne's married.
She's married to Peter.
They have two sons.
Their names are Bill and Jimmy.
They don't have any daughters.

Sylvia and Eileen aren't married.
Eileen's only fourteen.

John's married to Mary.
They have one son.
His name's Larry.

Sylvia has three nephews.
She doesn't have any nieces.

DAVID PARKER   JOAN PARKER

SYLVIA   BOB & EILEEN

PETER & ANN   JOHN & MARY

BILL   JIMMY   LARRY

PART THREE

David and Joan Parker have three grandsons.
They don't have any granddaughters.

Anne and Peter Wood have two sons.
They don't have any daughters.

Joan Parker is the same age as her husband.
John Parker is the same age as his wife.

Peter Wood is older than his wife.
He's one year older than her.

Eileen's younger than her brother.
She's five years younger than him.

Jimmy is younger than his brother.
Larry and Jimmy are the same age.

Drills

DRILL A (10) □ *T: Unit 3, Drill A. Listen!* □

1. **T:** How many children do Mr. and
   Mrs. Parker have? *Five.*
   T: They have five children.

   S: They have five children.
   S: They have five children.

2. **T:** How many daughters do they
   have? *Three.*
   T: They have three daughters.
   T: Now you do the same.

   S: They have three daughters.
   S: They have three daughters.

DRILL B (8) □ *T: Unit 3, Drill B. Listen!* □

1. **T:** Do Peter and Anne Wood have
   any children? *Yes/two sons.*
   T: Yes, they do. They have two
   sons.

   S: Yes, they do. They have two sons.
   S: Yes, they do. They have two sons.

2. **T:** Does Eileen have any nieces? *No.*
   T: No, she doesn't.
   T: Now you do the same.

   S: No, she doesn't.
   S: No, she doesn't.

DRILL C *(6)*   ☐ *T: Unit 3, Drill C. Listen!* ☐

1.   **T:** Sylvia is thirty and Anne is
      twenty-seven. *Sylvia*
    T: Sylvia is older than Anne.

                                 S: Sylvia is older than Anne.
                                   S: Sylvia is older than Anne.

2.   **T:** I'm thirty, and my husband is
      thirty-three. *I*
    T: I'm younger than my husband.
      T: Now you do the same.

                                     S: I'm younger than my husband.
                                   S: I'm younger than my husband.

Unit 3 □ *Text B*

A MEDICAL EXAMINATION FOR LIFE INSURANCE

PART ONE

Scene: Doctor Young's Office

Characters: Doctor Young, Mr. Wood

Dr. Young:	Come in, Mr. Wood.
Mr. Wood:	Thank you.
Dr. Y:	Sit down please. Now where's that form? Oh, here it is. Just a few routine questions. What's your full name?
Mr. W:	Peter Wood.
Dr. Y:	And your address?
Mr. W:	35 Central Avenue, Oceanside, Long Island, New York.
Dr. Y:	Date of birth?
Mr. W:	October twenty-first, nineteen thirty-five.
Dr. Y:	Are you married or single?
Mr. W:	I'm married.
Dr. Y:	Do you have any children?
Mr. W:	Yes. Two boys.

PART TWO

Dr. Y:	Is this your first application for Life Insurance?
Mr. W:	Yes, it is.
Dr. Y:	What do you do?
Mr. W:	I'm an engineer.
Dr. Y:	Are both your parents alive?
Mr. W:	Yes, they are.
Dr. Y:	Are they in good health?
Mr. W:	Yes.
Dr. Y:	Any history of mental illness in the family?
Mr. W:	No.
Dr. Y:	Good. Now — a few more questions about yourself. Do you smoke?
Mr. W:	No, I don't.

"DO YOU PLAY ANY SPORTS?"

"I PLAY TENNIS REGULARLY"

"I LIKE FISHING"

"I DRIVE A GREAT DEAL"

"JUST TAKE OFF YOUR SHIRT, PLEASE"

Dr. Y:	Wise man! Do you drink?
Mr. W:	A bit. Only in moderation.
Dr. Y:	What do you mean by 'only in moderation'?
Mr. W:	Oh, two or three beers a day, and a scotch now and then.
Dr. Y:	How much scotch do you drink in a week?
Mr. W:	About a third of a bottle.
Dr. Y:	Okay.

PART THREE

Dr. Y:	Now, let me see . . . Do you play any sports?
Mr. W:	Yes, I play tennis regularly.
Dr. Y:	Anything else?
Mr. W:	Well, I like fishing, but of course that's different.
Dr. Y:	Do you drive a car?
Mr. W:	Oh, yes, I drive a great deal.
Dr. Y:	Have you had any serious illnesses?
Mr. W:	No, I haven't.
Dr. Y:	What about your heart?
Mr. W:	Oh, my heart's all right.
Dr. Y:	Fine.
Mr. W:	Is that all?
Dr. Y:	Oh no! Just take your shirt off, please.

DRILL D *(8)*   □ *T: Unit 3, Drill D. Listen!* □

1. **T:** Do you drink? *No.*   **S:** No, I don't.
    T: No, I don't.   **S:** No, I don't.
2. **T:** Does your husband drink? *Yes/beer.*   **S:** Yes, he does. He drinks beer.
    T: Yes, he does. He drinks beer. **S:** Yes, he does. He drinks beer.
3. **T:** How much beer does he drink?
    Two or three beers a day.   **S:** He drinks two or three beers a day.
    T: He drinks two or three beers a day.   **S:** He drinks two or three beers a day.
    T: Now you do the same.

    New words: take; sugar; coffee; spoonful; spoonfuls; money

DRILL E *(32)*   □ *T: Unit 3, Drill E. Listen and repeat. (the) is optional.* □

1. **T:** January   17. **T:** January (the) first
2. **T:** February   18. **T:** January (the) second
3. **T:** March   19. **T:** January (the) third
4. **T:** April   20. **T:** January (the) fourth
5. **T:** May   21. **T:** January (the) fifth
6. **T:** June   22. **T:** February (the) sixth
7. **T:** July   23. **T:** February (the) seventh
8. **T:** August   24. **T:** March (the) eighth
9. **T:** September   25. **T:** March (the) ninth
10. **T:** October   26. **T:** March (the) tenth
11. **T:** November   27. **T:** April (the) eleventh
12. **T:** December   28. **T:** April (the) twelfth
13. **T:** January, February, March   29. **T:** May (the) thirteenth
14. **T:** April, May, June   30. **T:** May (the) twentieth
15. **T:** July, August, September   31. **T:** May (the) twenty-first
16. **T:** October, November, December   32. **T:** May (the) thirtieth

ORAL AND WRITTEN EXERCISES

EXERCISE A

Study this 'family tree':

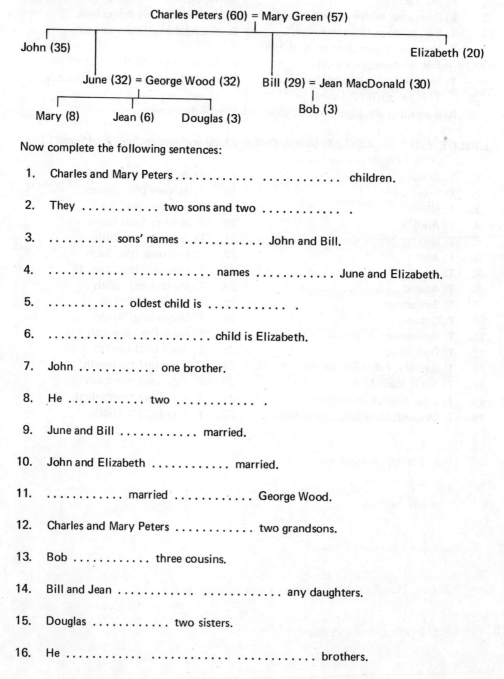

Now complete the following sentences:

1. Charles and Mary Peters . . . . children.

2. They . . . . two sons and two . . . .

3. . . . . sons' names . . . . John and Bill.

4. . . . . names . . . . June and Elizabeth.

5. . . . . oldest child is . . . .

6. . . . . child is Elizabeth.

7. John . . . . one brother.

8. He . . . . two . . . .

9. June and Bill . . . . married.

10. John and Elizabeth . . . . married.

11. . . . . married . . . . George Wood.

12. Charles and Mary Peters . . . . two grandsons.

13. Bob . . . . three cousins.

14. Bill and Jean . . . . any daughters.

15. Douglas . . . . two sisters.

16. He . . . . brothers.

17. Bob . . . . brothers or sisters.

18. Elizabeth . . . . two nephews and two . . . .

19. . . . . you . . . . any nephews?

20. No, I . . . . But I . . . . two . . . .

EXERCISE B

Study the family tree in Exercise A again.

Give questions for these answers. Example:

(a) *Do you have any sisters?*
     No, I don't have any sisters.

(b) *How many brothers do you have?*
     I have two brothers.

1.   . . . .
     They (Mr. and Mrs. Peters) have *four* children.

2.   . . . .
     Yes, they have two daughters.

3.   . . . .
     Their names are John and Bill.

4.   . . . .
     Yes. They (George and June Wood) have three children.

5.   . . . .
     No. They (Bill and Jean MacDonald) don't have any daughters.

6.   . . . .
     They have *four* grandchildren.

7.   . . . .
     I have *one* nephew.

8.   . . . .
     No. I don't have any nieces.

9.   . . . .
     No. They (The Parkers) don't have any granddaughters.

10. . . . .
     No. She (Elizabeth) isn't married.

EXERCISE C

Jean (18)

Wendy (19)

Carol (18)

Use the following words to complete the sentences:

(not) as . . . . as; older, younger; fat, fatter, fattest;
thin, thinner, thinnest; tall, taller, tallest;
the same . . . . (as); than.

1.   Jean is . . . .

2.   Wendy is . . . .

3.   Carol is . . . .

4.   Jean (18) is . . . . Wendy (19).

5.   Carol (18) is . . . . age . . . . Jean.

6.   She isn't . . . . age . . . . Wendy.

7.   Wendy is . . . . Jean, but she isn't . . . . tall
     . . . . Carol.

8.   Carol is the . . . . of the three girls.

9.   Wendy is the . . . . of the three girls.

10. Jean is the . . . . of the three girls.

11. Is Carol younger than Jean? No, she isn't. She's . . . . age.

12. Is Jean older than Wendy? No, she isn't. She's . . . .

13. Is Jean . . . . than Carol? Yes, she is.

14. Is Carol . . . . thin . . . . Wendy?

15. No, she isn't. But she's . . . . Jean.

EXERCISE D

Use *How much* or *How many* in these questions.

1. . . . . books do you have?

2. . . . . children do the Woods have?

3. . . . . scotch does he drink in a week?

4. . . . . sugar do you take in your coffee?

5. . . . . tennis rackets does Eileen have?

6. . . . . money do you have?

7. . . . . does Mr. Parker earn?

8. . . . . days a week does he go to New York?

9. . . . . cigarettes do you smoke a day?

10. . . . . cigarettes does Mr. Parker smoke a week?

EXERCISE E

Say and write these dates.

Examples:

(a) 4/10/58 *April (the) tenth, nineteen fifty-eight*

(b) 24 Dec. 1960 *December (the) twenty-fourth, nineteen sixty*

1. 10/6/59 . . . .

2. 6/10/67 . . . .

3. 1/11/39 . . . .

4. 3/1/46 . . . .

5. 8/3/72 . . . .

6. 12/22/64 . . . .

7. 5/2/42 . . . .

8. 9/2/39 . . . .

9. 2/5/15 . . . .

10. 7/8/73 . . . .

11. 8 Feb. 1968 . . . .

12. 12 Aug. 1973 . . . .

Unit 4 ☐ *Text A*

A VISIT TO THE PARKERS

PART ONE

Last Wednesday Hans and Lotte Volkers visited the Parkers.
They went to Elmhurst by train.
They arrived in Elmhurst at three o'clock.
David and Joan Parker were at the station, waiting for them.
David introduced the visitors to his wife.
Then they all walked to the Parkers' house.
The Parkers' house is very near the station, just across the park.
Joan walked with Lotte.
David walked with Hans, just behind the women.
They crossed the park and arrived at the house in five minutes.

DAVID INTRODUCED THE
VISITORS TO HIS WIFE

DAVID WALKED WITH HANS,
JUST BEHIND THE WOMEN

PART TWO

Hans and Lotte Volkers admired the house and the grounds.
They went in and sat down in the living room.
Joan asked her guests what they would like to drink.
Lotte said: "Coffee please! We like coffee very much."
Five minutes later Joan came into the room with the coffee.
"How do you take your coffee?" Joan asked Lotte.
"Just milk please, no sugar," Lotte replied.
"But Hans likes his black," she added.
Joan poured the coffee.
Then she offered cake and cookies to her guests.

HANS AND LOTTE VOLKERS ADMIRED
THE HOUSE AND GROUNDS

"...HANS LIKES HIS BLACK"

PART THREE

After coffee, Joan offered to show her guests the house.
First she showed them the bedrooms, upstairs.
Then she showed them the dining room and the kitchen.
Later they all got into the car and drove around the town.
First they drove to the center of town.
Joan pointed out the stores to Lotte.
Then David pointed out the football stadium to Hans.
"Unfortunately", he said, "it's closed for the season."
Later, David drove his guests back to their hotel.
The Volkers had a dinner appointment at seven-thirty.

FIRST SHE SHOWED
THEM THE BEDROOMS

THEY DROVE AROUND THE TOWN

DAVID DROVE HIS GUESTS BACK TO THEIR HOTEL

PART FOUR

Hans and Lotte Volkers didn't visit the Parkers last Thursday; they visited them last
   Wednesday.
They didn't go to Elmhurst by car; they went by train.
They didn't arrive in Elmhurst at four o'clock; they arrived there at three o'clock.
They didn't drive to the Parkers' house; they walked there.
Joan didn't walk with Hans; she walked with Lotte.
They didn't sit in the kitchen; they sat in the living room.
Lotte didn't say "Tea please"; she said "Coffee, please".
David didn't pour the coffee; Joan poured it.
Joan didn't show her guests the kitchen first; she showed them the bedrooms first.
The Volkers returned to their hotel by car; they didn't return by train.

Drills

DRILL A *(7)*   ☐ *T: Unit 4, Drill A. Listen!* ☐

1.   **T:** Did Hans and Lotte Volkers visit the
       Parkers last Wednesday? *Yes.*   **S:** Yes, they did.
     T: Yes, they did.   **S:** Yes, they did.
2.   **T:** Did they visit the Parkers last
       Tuesday? *No/last Wednesday.*   **S:** No, they didn't. They visited them last
                                                    Wednesday.
     T: No, they didn't. They visited them
     last Wednesday.   **S:** No, they didn't. They visited them last
       T: Now you do the same.   Wednesday.
     New words: Tuesday; bus; eat.

DRILL B *(10)*   ☐ *T: Unit 4, Drill B. Listen!* ☐

1.   **T:** Did you take the train?   **S:** Did you take the train?
     T: Did you take the train?   **S:** Did you take the train?
2.   **T:** *the bus?*   **S:** Did you take the bus?
     T: Did you take the bus?   **S:** Did you take the bus?
3.   **T:** Did she have a cup of coffee?   **S:** Did she have a cup of coffee?
     T: Did she have a cup of coffee?   **S:** Did she have a cup of coffee?
4.   **T:** *a cup of tea?*   **S:** Did she have a cup of tea?
     T: Did she have a cup of tea?   **S:** Did she have a cup of tea?
       T: Now you do the same.
     New words: cup; cookie

DRILL C *(7)*   ☐ *T: Unit 4, Drill C. Listen!* ☐

1.   **T:** They visited the Parkers last week.
       When?   **S:** When did they visit the Parkers?
     T: When did they visit the Parkers?   **S:** When did they visit the Parkers?
2.   **T:** They went to Elmhurst by train.
       How?   **S:** How did they go to Elmhurst?
     T: How did they go to Elmhurst?   **S:** How did they go to Elmhurst?
3.   **T:** She arrived in the United States
       last month. *When?*   **S:** When did she arrive in the United
                                                    States?
     T: When did she arrive in the United
     States?   **S:** When did she arrive in the United
                                                    States?
       T: Now you do the same.
     New words: month; yesterday; (last) night; theater; supper; movies; (last) week

DRILL D *(8)*   □ *T: Unit 4, Drill D. Listen!* □

1.   T: Was David at the station when the
        Volkers arrived? *Yes.*   S: Yes, he was.
     T: Yes, he was.   S: Yes, he was.
2.   T: Was Eileen there too? *No/at school.*   S: No, she wasn't. She was at school.
     T: No, she wasn't. She was at school.   S: No, she wasn't. She was at school.
3.   T: Were they in New York last week?
        Yes   S: Yes, they were.
     T: Yes, they were.   S: Yes, they were.
4.   T: Were you in San Francisco last
        month? *No/in Los Angeles.*   S: No, I wasn't. I was in Los Angeles.
     T: No, I wasn't. I was in Los Angeles.   S: No, I wasn't. I was in Los Angeles.
     T: Now you do the same.
   New words: open; o'clock; shut; strong.

DRILL E *(4)*   □ *T: Unit 4, Drill E. Listen!* □

1.   T: What did David say? *This is my wife.*   S: He said: "This is my wife."
     T: He said: "This is my wife."   S: He said: "This is my wife."
2.   T: Where did they drive first? *To the
        center of town.*   S: They drove to the center of town.
     T: They drove to the center of town.   S: They drove to the center of town.
     T: Now you do the same.

Unit 4 □ *Text B*

ON VACATION

Time: 8:15 a.m., mid-August

Characters: Peter Wood; Bill Porter

PART ONE

Bill:	Morning, Peter!
Peter:	Morning, Bill!
Bill:	Oh, well. Back to the rat race.
Peter:	Yes, I'm afraid so.
Bill:	Still, it was good while it lasted.
Peter:	How was the weather?
Bill:	It was wonderful.
Peter:	Didn't you have any rain?
Bill:	No. We had blue skies every day.
Peter:	What did the children do?
Bill:	They played on the beach the whole day.
Peter:	Were you with them the whole time?
Bill:	No. We were lucky. We met a nice couple who had two children exactly the same age as ours.
Peter:	I see.
Bill:	So we took care of all the children on alternate days.
Peter:	That was a good arrangement.
Bill:	Yes. In that way we all had several days of complete freedom. It was marvellous.

"OH, WELL. BACK TO THE RAT RACE"

"WE WERE LUCKY"

49

PART TWO

Bill:	What about you? You look pretty sunburnt.
Peter:	We cheated, I'm afraid.
Bill:	Oh? How?
Peter:	Anne's sister, Eileen, came with us and took care of the children most days.
Bill:	Where did you go?
Peter:	We went to Maine.
Bill:	Where did you stay?
Peter:	In a motel, about twenty miles from Portland.
Bill:	How did you hear about it?
Peter:	Anne's parents stayed there last year.
Bill:	So you knew all about the place before you went?
Peter:	Yes.
Bill:	Was the motel comfortable?
Peter:	It was all right.
Bill:	What about food?
Peter:	There was a small kitchen in our room, so we were able to do our own cooking.
Bill:	I see.
Peter:	But we went out to a restaurant at least once a day.

"IN A MOTEL, ABOUT TWENTY
MILES FROM PORTLAND"

PART THREE

Bill:	Are there any good restaurants in that part of Maine?
Peter:	There are some marvellous seafood restaurants.
Bill:	Was there much traffic on the roads?
Peter:	There was quite a bit, but compared with New York the roads were empty.
Bill:	Was there a beach nearby?
Peter:	No. The nearest was about six miles away.
Bill:	Did you get a chance to swim, then?
Peter:	No. The water's too cold for me in Maine.
Bill:	Did you do any sailing?
Peter:	Sailing? No!
Bill:	Did you do any mountain climbing?
Peter:	You must be kidding!
Bill:	Did you play any tennis, then?
Peter:	Just enough.
Bill:	What do you mean 'Just enough'?
Peter:	Just enough to work up a nice thirst for the cocktail hour!

"JUST ENOUGH...."   "...TO WORK UP A NICE THIRST"

DRILL F *(32)*   □ *T: Unit 4, Drill F. Listen and repeat* □

1.	**T:** There's a beach nearby.	**S:**	(There's a beach nearby.)
2.	**T:** There's a hotel nearby.	**S:**	(There's a hotel nearby.)
3.	**T:** There's a motel near the station.	**S:**	(There's a motel near the station.)
4.	**T:** There's a train in the station.	**S:**	(There's a train in the station.)
5.	**T:** There's a car on the road.	**S:**	(There's a car on the road.)
6.	**T:** There's some coffee in the cup.	**S:**	(There's some coffee in the cup.)
7.	**T:** There's some tea in the cup.	**S:**	(There's some tea in the cup.)
8.	**T:** There was a beach nearby.	**S:**	(There was a beach nearby.)

9.	**T:** There was a hotel nearby.	**S:** (There was a hotel nearby.)
10.	**T:** There was a motel near the beach.	**S:** (There was a motel near the beach.)
11.	**T:** There was a train in the station.	**S:** (There was a train in the station.)
12.	**T:** There was a car on the road.	**S:** (There was a car on the road.)
13.	**T:** There was some coffee in the cup.	**S:** (There was some coffee in the cup.)
14.	**T:** There was some tea in the cup.	**S:** (There was some tea in the cup.)
15.	**T:** There were some hotels nearby.	**S:** (There were some hotels nearby.)
16.	**T:** There were some motels near the beach.	**S:** (There were some motels near the beach.)
17.	**T:** There were some cars on the road.	**S:** (There were some cars on the road.)
18.	**T:** There isn't any coffee in this cup.	**S:** (There isn't any coffee in this cup.)
19.	**T:** There isn't any tea in this cup.	**S:** (There isn't any tea in this cup.)
20.	**T:** There aren't any beaches nearby.	**S:** (There aren't any beaches nearby.)
21.	**T:** There aren't any hotels nearby.	**S:** (There aren't any hotels nearby.)
22.	**T:** There aren't any cars on the road.	**S:** (There aren't any cars on the road.)
23.	**T:** There wasn't any coffee in the cup.	**S:** (There wasn't any coffee in the cup.)
24.	**T:** There wasn't any tea in the cup.	**S:** (There wasn't any tea in the cup.)
25.	**T:** There weren't any beaches nearby.	**S:** (There weren't any beaches nearby.)
26.	**T:** There weren't any hotels nearby.	**S:** (There weren't any hotels nearby.)
27.	**T:** There weren't any cars on the road.	**S:** (There weren't any cars on the road.)
28.	**T:** Is there a beach nearby?	**S:** (Is there a beach nearby?)
29.	**T:** Is there any coffee in the cup?	**S:** (Is there any coffee in the cup?)
30.	**T:** Was there a train in the station?	**S:** (Was there a train in the station?)
31.	**T:** Was there any coffee in the cup?	**S:** (Was there any coffee in the cup?)
32.	**T:** Were there any motels near the beach?	**S:** (Were there any motels near the beach?)

ORAL AND WRITTEN EXERCISES

EXERCISE A

Complete these sentences, using the past tense of the verb given in the parentheses:

1. Miss Jones . . . . me to her sister. (introduce)

2. The two girls . . . . to the station. (walk)

3. The men . . . . the park. (cross)

4. Mr. Parker . . . . his friend a cigarette. (offer)

5. "Do you smoke cigars?", he . . . . me. (ask)

6. "Yes, I do", I . . . . (reply)

7. I . . . . my grandmother last week. (visit)

8. I . . . . by bus to the center of town and . . . . off near her house. (go; get)

9. Our friends . . . . us if we would like to see their new car. (ask)

10. We all . . . . it. (admire)

11. Joan . . . . the coffee into the living room. (bring)

12. She . . . . the coffee. (pour)

13. After coffee they . . . . in the back yard. (sit)

14. Joan . . . . her guests around the house. (show)

15. Lotte . . . . : "I like your house very much, Joan." (say)

16. We . . . . around the town in David's car. (drive)

17. First, we . . . . to the center of town. (go)

18. I . . . . out the stores to my friend. (point)

19. We . . . . to the hotel by car. (return)

20. We . . . . at the hotel before seven o'clock. (arrive)

EXERCISE B

Put these sentences into the interrogative form.

Example: Peter and Anne visited their friends, Edward and Carol, in Boston.

*Did Peter and Anne visit their
friends, Edward and Carol, in Boston?*

Begin each question with the word *Did.*

1. They went there by car.

    . . . .

2. They arrived there before twelve o'clock.

    . . . .

3. They looked at Boston harbor.

    . . . .

4. They had lunch in a restaurant.

    . . . .

5. After lunch, Anne went shopping with Carol.

    . . . .

6. Peter and Edward went to a football game.

    . . . .

7. After the game, Peter met some old friends in a bar.

    . . . .

8. He had several drinks with his friends.

    . . . .

9. Anne drove the car back to New York.

    . . . .

EXERCISE C

Put these sentences into the negative:

1. The good weather lasted all week.

    . . . .

2. It rained every day.

    . . . .

3. They had blue skies every day.

    . . . .

4. The children played on the beach the whole day.

    . . . .

5. We stayed at a hotel.

    . . . .

6. We took care of the children every day.

    . . . .

7. Their children were the same age as ours.

    . . . .

8. We left the children with their grandparents. (Note: the base form of *left* is *leave*)

    . . . .

9. Peter and Anne went to Canada.

    . . . .

10. The motel was very comfortable.

    . . . .

EXERCISE D

Answer these questions as in the example:

Did you go to Maine last year? No/to Canada.

No, I didn't. I went to Canada.

1. Did Joan Parker offer beer to her guests? No/coffee.

    . . . .

2. Did the Volkers visit them (the Parkers) last Monday? No/last Wednesday.

    . . . .

3. Did they go to Elmhurst by car? No/by train.

    . . . .

4. Did they have coffee in the back yard? No/in the living room.

    . . . .

5. Did Lotte say "We don't like coffee"? No/"We like coffee very much".

    . . . .

6. Did David pour the coffee? No/Joan.

    . . . .

7. Did Joan point out the football stadium to Hans? No/David.

    . . . .

8. Did you go to a nightclub last night? No/to the movies.

    No, I . . . . I . . . .

9. Did you go to Mexico last year? No/to Canada.

    No, I . . . . I . . . .

10. Did you stay in a motel? No/a hotel.

    No, we . . . . We . . . .

EXERCISE E

Give questions for the answers.

Example:

Where did your friends go last year?

They (My friends) went to Mexico last year. (Where)

1. ....

   They (The children) played on the beach. (Where)

2. ....

   We went there (to Boston) by car. (How)

3. ....

   She (Joan) offered them (her guests) cake and cookies. (What)

4. ....

   No, there weren't many good restaurants near the beach. (Were)

5. ....

   She (Lotte) said: "No, thanks; I don't smoke." (What)

6. ....

   We arrived in Boston before lunch. (When)

7. ....

   I arrived here last Monday. (When)

8. ....

   She (Joan) asked Lotte: "Do you have any children?" (What)

9. ....

   They drove to the center of town. (Where)

10. ....

    They left their hotel at two o'clock. (What time)

11. ....

    They had lunch in a restaurant. (Where)

Unit 5 □ *Text A*

THE NEWS

PART ONE

This is WNYC, New York. It's one o'clock and time for the news.

A military plane has crashed in California.
It crashed only half an hour ago.
There haven't been any details yet.

The Los Angeles Dodgers have won the World Series.

The Russians have announced a new success in space.
Their space-craft transmitted pictures of Mars at about 10 o'clock last night.
American scientists have picked up signals from the space-craft.

The President has accepted an invitation to visit Japan.
He has not previously been to Japan.

The sit-in at a Detroit high school has ended.
It began last Thursday when the principal expelled a student for smoking marijuana.

Arthur Colson, a twenty-eight year old engineer from Boston, has flown across the
   Atlantic in a balloon.
He reached the Irish coast at 9 o'clock this morning.

The Ford Motor Company has decided to build another factory in Germany.

That's the end of the news. Stay tuned for the weather report.

Drills

DRILL A *(9)*   □ *T: Unit 5, Drill A. Listen!* □

1. **T:** A plane has crashed near Los
       Angeles.
                                    S: A plane has crashed near Los
                                       Angeles.

    T: A plane has crashed near Los
       Angeles.
                                    S: A plane has crashed near Los
                                       Angeles.

2. **T:** *A train.*   **S:** A train has crashed near Los Angeles.
    T: A train has crashed near Los Angeles. **S:** A train has crashed near Los Angeles.

3.   T: The Russians have announced a   S: The Russians have announced a
         new success in space.   new success in space.
      T: The Russians have announced a   S: The Russians have announced a
         new success in space.   new success in space.
4.   T: *The Americans.*   S: The Americans have announced a
                                                    new success in space.
      T: The Americans have announced a   S: The Americans have announced a
         new success in space.   new success in space.
         T: Now you do the same.

DRILL B *(7)*   □ *T: Unit 5, Drill B. Listen!* □

1.   T: Has the President accepted an
         invitation to visit Japan? *Yes.*   S: Yes, he has.
      T: Yes, he has.   S: Yes, he has.
2.   T: Has he accepted an invitation to
         visit Australia? *No/Japan*   S: No, he hasn't. He's accepted an
                                                    invitation to visit Japan
      T: No, he hasn't. He's accepted an
         invitation to visit Japan.   S: No, he hasn't. He's accepted an
                                                    invitation to visit Japan.
3.   T: Have your friends been to Belgium?
         No.   S: No, they haven't.
      T: No, they haven't.   S: No, they haven't.
         T: Now you do the same.

DRILL C *(6)*   □ *T: Unit 5, Drill C. Listen!* □

1.   T: What has crashed in California?   S: A military plane has crashed in
         A military plane   California.
      T: A military plane has crashed in
         California.   S: A military plane has crashed in
                                                    California.
2.   T: What have the Russians announced?
         A new success in space.   S: The Russians have announced a new
                                                    success in space.
      T: The Russians have announced a new
         success in space.   S: The Russians have announced a new
                                                    success in space.
         T: Now you do the same.

Unit 5 □ *Text B*

THE PARKERS AT BREAKFAST

PART ONE

David:	Has the mailman come yet, Bob?
Bob:	Yes. There were only two letters — one for you and Mother, and one for me.
Eileen:	Nothing for me?
Bob:	Of course not.
Eileen:	Why 'of course not'?
Bob:	Well, you never write to anyone. You've never written a letter in your life.
Eileen:	I have.
Bob:	You haven't.
Joan:	Now you two, stop arguing and eat your breakfast.

PART TWO

David:	Who was our letter from, Joan?
Joan:	Anne. Here it is.
David:	Have you read it?
Joan:	Yes.
David:	Well, just tell me what she says.
Joan:	Don't you want to read it?
David:	I've left my glasses in the bedroom. Have they moved yet?
Joan:	Yes. They moved last Tuesday.
David:	How do they like the new house?
Joan:	They love it.
David:	Good.
Joan:	They've bought one or two new pieces of furniture.
David:	Have they got rid of that awful old sofa?
Joan:	Yes. And they've bought some new chairs for the den.

PART THREE

David: Have they begun to paint the kitchen?

Joan: Yes. They started on that last weekend.

David: I suppose they've also painted the front hall?

Joan: Yes. But they haven't touched the bedrooms yet.

David: Well, at least they've made a start.

Joan: They've been very lucky with their neighbors.

David: In what way have they been lucky?

Joan: Well, they were very kind on the day Anne moved.

David: What did they do?

Joan: Sarah — that's the wife's name — took care of the two boys the whole day.

David: That was nice of her!

Joan: . . . and Tom — that's the husband — helped Peter lay the carpets.

David: Did he?

Joan: He's even offered to help Peter paint the bedrooms.

"THEY'VE BEEN VERY LUCKY WITH THEIR NEIGHBORS"

PART FOUR

Eileen:	Why doesn't Bob go and help them?
Bob:	No thank you. I've got my own problems.
Eileen:	Such as?
Bob:	Mind your own business.
Eileen:	Such as taking that glamorous blond out every night.
Bob:	Don't you say anything about Georgia. She's . . . .
Joan:	Now then, you two. Stop it right now.
David:	By the way, Bob. I want you to help me wash the car this evening.
Bob:	Oh, Dad. Not this evening.
David:	Why not?
Bob:	Well, I've promised . . . .
Eileen:	. . . . to take Georgia out.
Bob:	Oh shut up, Eileen.
David:	Tell me Bob. Is Georgia a strong girl?
Bob:	She certainly is.
David:	Then invite her for dinner. She can help us both wash the car!

"THEN INVITE HER FOR DINNER"

DRILL D *(10)*   □ *T: Unit 5, Drill D. Listen and repeat.* □

1. **T:** I want to speak French.
2. **T:** I don't want to speak English.
3. **T:** She wants to speak Spanish.
4. **T:** She doesn't want to speak English.
5. **T:** He wants to speak German.
6. **T:** He doesn't want to speak French
7. **T:** Peter wants to go to Canada.
8. **T:** He doesn't want to go to Mexico.
9. **T:** We want to go to the movies.
10. **T:** We don't want to go to the theater.

DRILL E *(10)*   □ *T: Unit 5, Drill E. Listen and repeat.* □

1. **T:** I want you to speak English.
2. **T:** I don't want you to speak Spanish.
3. **T:** My father wants me to help him today.
4. **T:** He doesn't want me to help him tomorrow.
5. **T:** We want our son to visit Yale.
6. **T:** We don't want him to visit Harvard.
7. **T:** My parents want me to become a doctor.
8. **T:** They don't want me to become a lawyer.
9. **T:** Mr. Parker wants Eileen to learn German.
10. **T:** He doesn't want her to learn Latin.

New words: Harvard; Yale; parents; Latin; lawyer; become.

DRILL F *(6)*   □ *T: Unit 5, Drill F. Listen!* □

1. **T:** Do you want to stay at home? *Yes.*   **S:** Yes, I do.
    T: Yes, I do.   **S:** Yes, I do.
2. **T:** Does Joan want to go to the theater?
    No/to the movies.   **S:** No she doesn't. She wants to go to the movies.

    T: Now you do the same.
New words: newspaper; like (v); learn.

DRILL G *(17)*

What time is it?

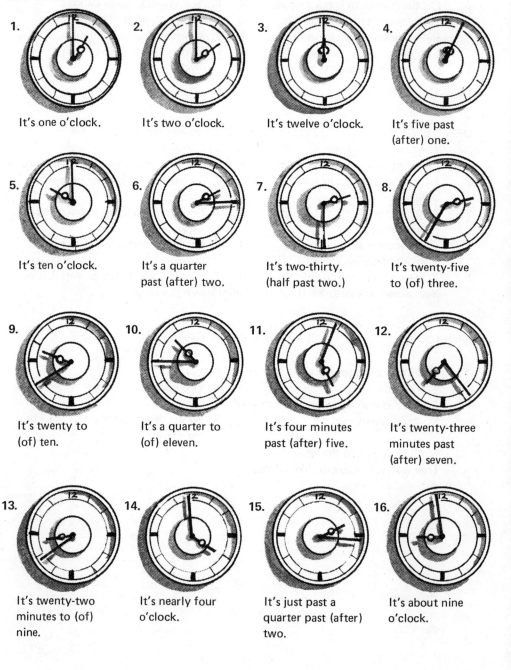

1. It's one o'clock.

2. It's two o'clock.

3. It's twelve o'clock.

4. It's five past (after) one.

5. It's ten o'clock.

6. It's a quarter past (after) two.

7. It's two-thirty. (half past two.)

8. It's twenty-five to (of) three.

9. It's twenty to (of) ten.

10. It's a quarter to (of) eleven.

11. It's four minutes past (after) five.

12. It's twenty-three minutes past (after) seven.

13. It's twenty-two minutes to (of) nine.

14. It's nearly four o'clock.

15. It's just past a quarter past (after) two.

16. It's about nine o'clock.

ORAL AND WRITTEN EXERCISES

EXERCISE A

Rewrite the following sentences beginning with the word given in parentheses:

Example: A military plane has crashed in California. (Where)

Where has a military plane crashed?

1.   The plane crashed only half an hour ago. (When)

. . . .

2.   The Los Angeles Dodgers have won the World Series. (What)

. . . .

3.   The Russians have announced a new success in space. (What)

. . . .

4.   Their space-craft transmitted pictures of Mars at about 10 o'clock last night. (When)

. . . .

5.   The President has accepted an invitation to visit Japan. (Who)

. . . .

6.   The sit-in began last Thursday. (When)

. . . .

7.   A student was expelled for smoking marijuana. (Why)

. . . .

8.   Arthur Colson has flown across the Atlantic in a balloon. (Who)

. . . .

9.   He left Nova Scotia five days ago. (When)

. . . .

10.   He reached the Irish coast at 9 o'clock this morning. (When)

. . . .

EXERCISE B

Complete these sentences with the simple past or the present perfect tense of the verb given in parentheses after each. Where *just* is given, place it correctly.

Note these irregular verbs and their principal forms: see, saw, seen; be, was, been; swim, swam, swum; drive, drove, driven; win, won, won.

1. I . . . . from Boston last night. (return).

2. Hans . . . . the Parkers last Wednesday. (visit)

3. My sister . . . . home from Canada. (just/arrive)

4. . . . . you . . . . many cars on the road when you . . . .
   in Maine? (see; be)

5. We . . . . the news that British scientists . . . . signals from
   our new space-craft. (just/receive; pick up)

6. What time . . . . the plane . . . .? (crash)

7. A: . . . . you . . . . your lunch? B: Not yet. (have)

8. . . . . the sit-in . . . . today or yesterday? (end)

9. Arthur Colson . . . . n't . . . . the Atlantic last year. (fly)

10. Mr. Parker . . . . to the center of town. (just/drive)

11. . . . . he . . . . the Volkers to their hotel? (drive)

    Yes, he . . . .

12. Who . . . . the World Series last year? (win)

EXERCISE C

Rewrite these sentences in the negative.

Example: John wants to study Latin.

John doesn't want to study Latin.

1. They want to go for a walk in the park.

   . . . .

2. The children want to play on the beach.

   . . . .

3.   David and Joan want to go to the movies this evening.

. . . .

4.   David wants Joan to watch a Western.

. . . .

5.   They want us to arrive before dinner.

. . . .

6.   John wants you to see him at his office.

. . . .

7.   The children's mother wants them to play on the beach.

. . . .

8.   Do you want me to read the next sentence?

. . . .

9.   Yes, I do. . . . .

10.   Does David want to go to Mexico this year?

. . . .

11.   Yes, he does. . . . .

12.   He wanted his son to drive the car.

. . . .

13.   I wanted to visit Princeton.

. . . .

14.   They wanted us to stay for dinner.

. . . .

15.   She wanted to show them the house.

. . . .

EXERCISE D

Rephrase these sentences as in the example:

Please wait in the next room.

I want you to wait in the next room, please.

1. Please call me at seven o'clock.

. . . .

2. Please help me do this exercise.

. . . .

3. Please help me get lunch ready.

. . . .

4. Please introduce me to your friends.

. . . .

5. Please ask your sister to play tennis with us.

. . . .

6. Please tell me your name and address.

. . . .

7. Please take care of the children today.

. . . .

8. Please drive Hans to his hotel.

. . . .

9. Please show them the back yard.

. . . .

10. Please meet my friends at the station.

. . . .

EXERCISE E

What time is it?

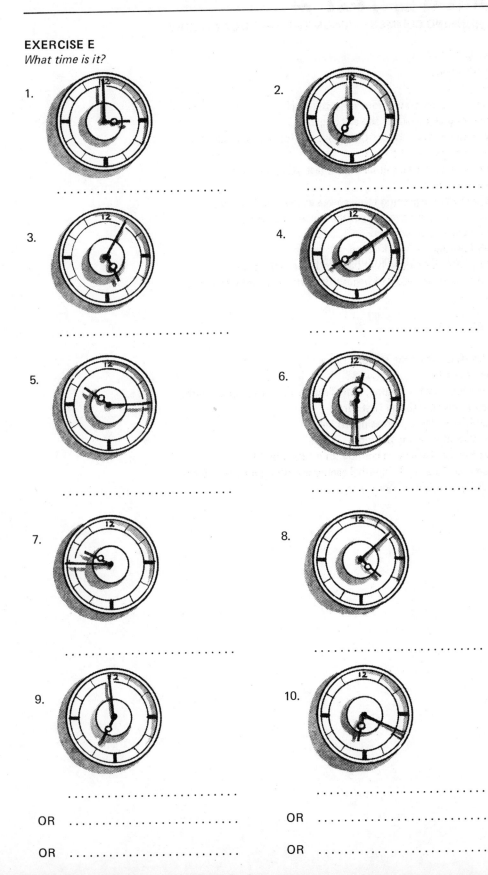

1.

. . . .

2.

. . . .

3.

. . . .

4.

. . . .

5.

. . . .

6.

. . . .

7.

. . . .

8.

. . . .

9.

. . . .

OR . . . .

OR . . . .

10.

. . . .

OR . . . .

OR . . . .

Unit 6 □ *Text A*

A RUNNING COMMENTARY ON THE KENTUCKY DERBY

PART ONE

The horses are coming out onto the track.
They're going towards the starting gate.
Here comes Lazy Student, the favorite for today's race.
He's looking very fit.
And here comes Grammar Rules, last year's winner.
He's wearing blinkers.
Now they're beginning to assemble at the starting gate.
The trainers are trying to get the horses into the stalls.
Homework is objecting.
He's backing out and kicking.
The jockey is coaxing him back into the stall again.
And now we're ready to begin this year's Kentucky Derby.

PART TWO

We're waiting for the starting signal.
They're off!
Grammar Rules is leading, with Translation close behind him.
They're coming to the first turn.
Grammar Rules is increasing his lead.
Translation is falling behind.
And English Teacher is coming up on the outside.
Grammar Rules and English Teacher are running neck and neck.
At this point it's anybody's race.

PART THREE

Now English Teacher is going into the lead.
Grammar Rules is beginning to tire.
But Lazy Student is moving up on the inside rail.
He's gaining ground.
He's catching up with the leaders.
Now he's coming into second place.
They're nearing the finishing line.
Lazy Student is overtaking English Teacher.
He's increasing his lead.
And Lazy Student is the winner by two lengths over English Teacher.

"AT THIS POINT IT'S ANYBODY'S RACE."

Unit 6 □ *Text B*

A CONVERSATION ABOUT THE KENTUCKY DERBY

PART ONE

Bill: Did you see the Kentucky Derby this afternoon, Peter?
Peter: Yes, I saw it on television.
Bill: Who won?
Peter: Lazy Student, the favorite. But Grammar Rules was leading for most of the race.
Bill: What happened to him?
Peter: He began to tire as they came into the last turn.
Bill: How much was he leading by?
Peter: He was neck and neck with English Teacher.
Bill: What happened to English Teacher?
Peter: He held on to the lead until the last moment and then he was beaten at the post.

PART TWO

Bill: One of the horses was racing in blinkers, I believe?
Peter: Yes, Grammar Rules, last year's winner.
Bill: How many horses were running?
Peter: About twenty, I think.
Bill: Who was riding the winner?
Peter: I don't know. I didn't get his name.
Bill: What did he win by?
Peter: He won by two lengths.
Bill: Was he running well at the finish?
Peter: Yes, he was still increasing his lead.

Unit 6 □ *Text C*

THE WEEKEND

PART ONE

Peter:	What are you going to do this weekend, Bill?
Bill:	I'm going to have a good rest.
Peter:	You're not going to play golf, then?
Bill:	No. I'm staying at home.
Peter:	The weather's absolutely perfect for a round of golf.
Bill:	I know; but Jean's parents are coming to see us on Sunday.
Peter:	What about tomorrow?
Bill:	Well, Jean's having her hair done tomorrow morning.
Peter:	And you're going to take care of the kids, I suppose.
Bill:	That's right!
Peter:	I thought you said you were having a rest.
Bill:	Oh, the boys aren't much trouble. They'll play in the back yard while I'm washing the dishes and making the beds.

PART TWO

Peter:	After that, I suppose you'll make lunch.
Bill:	As a matter of fact, I *am* making lunch tomorrow.
Peter:	Good Lord!
Bill:	Oh, it won't be all that bad.
Peter:	Why?
Bill:	Because I'm going to peel the potatoes tonight.
Peter:	What are you doing tomorrow afternoon?
Bill:	I'm going to put a new muffler on the car.
Peter:	Is that your idea of a rest?
Bill:	Certainly. They say a change is as good as a rest, don't they?

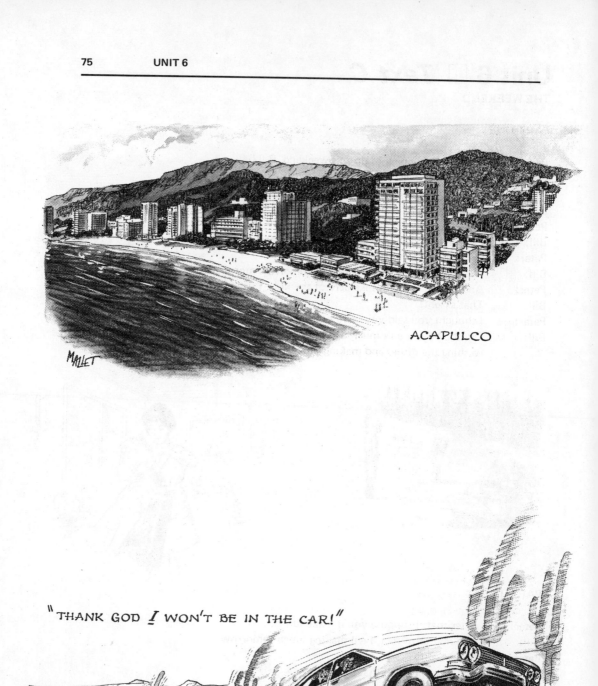

ACAPULCO

"THANK GOD _I_ WON'T BE IN THE CAR!"

PART THREE

Bill: What are *you* doing this weekend, Peter?
Peter: We're probably going to see Anne's folks.
Bill: Oh, yes? How are they?
Peter: They're fine. They're going on vacation next week.
Bill: Where are they going?
Peter: They're going to Mexico.
Bill: Mexico City?
Peter: Yes, they're going to Mexico City *first*, I think.
Bill: Are they going to Acapulco?
Peter: Yes; they're going there too, I think.
Bill: When are they leaving?
Peter: Next Thursday.
Bill: How long are they going to be in Mexico?
Peter: About three weeks.
Bill: Are they flying?
Peter: No. They're going by car.
Bill: I suppose Bob'll do some of the driving?
Peter: Yes. Thank God *I* won't be in the car!

Drills

DRILL A *(8)*  □ *T: Unit 6, Drill A. Listen!* □

1. **Picture number one.**
T: Is Mr. Parker smoking a
cigarette or a cigar?
S: He's smoking a cigarette.

2. **Picture number two.**
T: Are these men working or playing
tennis?
S: They're playing tennis.
T: Now you do the same.

3. **Picture number three.**

4. **Picture number four.**

5. **Picture number five.**

6. **Picture number six.**

7. **Picture number seven.**

8. **Picture number eight.**

DRILL B *(9)*   □ *Unit 6, Drill B. Look at the pictures on page 77 again.*
Listen! □

1.   **T:** Picture number one.
      Does Mr. Parker drive a car.   **S:** Yes, he does.
     T: Yes, he does.   **S:** Yes, he does.
2.   **T:** Is Mr. Parker driving a car now? **S:** No, he isn't.
     T: No, he isn't.   **S:** No, he isn't.
3.   **T:** What's he doing now?   **S:** He's smoking a cigarette.
     T: He's smoking a cigarette.   **S:** He's smoking a cigarette.
        T: Now you do the same.

DRILL C *(5)*   □ *T: Unit 6, Drill C. Listen!* □

1.   **T:** What's Bob doing tomorrow?
      Visiting a friend.   **S:** He's visiting a friend.
     T: He's visiting a friend.   **S:** He's visiting a friend.
2.   **T:** What are doing this evening?
      Working.   **S:** I'm working.
     T: I'm working.   **S:** I'm working.
        T: Now you do the same.

DRILL D *(5)*   □ *T: Unit 6, Drill D. Listen!* □

1.   **T:** What's Bob going to do tomorrow?
      Visit a friend.   **S:** He's going to visit a friend.
     T: He's going to visit a friend.   **S:** He's going to visit a friend.
        T: Now you do the same.

ORAL AND WRITTEN EXERCISES

EXERCISE A   Answer the following questions about these pictures.

Picture number 1:

(a)   Are these women admiring a house?   . . . .

(b)   What are they doing?   . . . .

Picture number 2:

(a)   Is David working in the department store?   . . . .

(b)   What is he doing?   . . . .

Picture number 3:

(a)   Is Bob playing tennis?   . . . .

(b)   What is he doing? . . . .

Picture number 4:

(a)   Is Joan waiting for a train? . . . .

(b)   What is she doing? . . . .

Picture number 5:

(a)   Are these men training their horses? . . . .

(b)   W hat are they doing? . . . .

Picture number 6:

(a)   Are these children playing in a park?   . . . .

(b)   What are they doing? . . . .

EXERCISE B

Write out fifteen questions from Table 1 and fifteen answers from Table 2.

Example: Q: What's Jean going to do this evening?
         A: She's going to have a nap.

Table 1

What's	Peter Bill Jean he she	going to do	tomorrow? on Tuesday? this evening? tonight? tomorrow morning? now?
What're	Mr. and Mrs. Parker they you we		

Table 2

I'm He's She's We're They're	going to	visit a friend. work in the house. make the beds. peel the potatoes. get some money from the bank. buy me (etc.) a book. show me (etc.) some photographs. have dinner in town. have a nap.

1. Q: . . . . ?

   A: . . . .

2. Q: . . . . ?

   A: . . . .

3. Q: . . . . ?

   A: . . . .

4. Q: . . . . ?

   A: . . . .

5. Q: . . . . ?

   A: . . . .

6. Q: . . . . ?

   A: . . . .

7. Q: .... ?

A: ....

8. Q: .... ?

A: ....

9. Q: .... ?

A: ....

10. Q: .... ?

A: ....

11. Q: .... ?

A: ....

12. Q: .... ?

A: ....

13. Q: .... ?

A: ....

14. Q: .... ?

A: ....

15. Q: .... ?

A: ....

EXERCISE C

Write out ten questions from Table 1 and ten answers from Table 2.

Table 1

What's	Peter Bill Jean he she	doing	tomorrow? on Tuesday? next week? on Saturday night? tonight? tomorrow morning?
What're	Mr. and Mrs. Parker they you we		

Table 2

I'm He's She's We're They're	visiting a friend. painting the kitchen. going to the library. going on their (etc.) vacation. driving to New York. washing the car. fixing the radio. having her (etc.) hair done.

1. Q: . . . . ?

    A: . . . .

2. Q: . . . . ?

    A: . . . .

3. Q: . . . . ?

    A: . . . .

4. Q: . . . . ?

    A: . . . .

5. Q: . . . . ?

    A. . . . .

6. Q: . . . . ?

    A: . . . .

7. Q: . . . . ?

    A: . . . .

8. Q: . . . . ?

    A: . . . .

9. Q: . . . . ?

    A: . . . .

10. Q: . . . . ?

    A: . . . .

EXERCISE D

Put the following sentences into the negative.

1. Lazy Student is wearing blinkers for today's race.

    . . . .

2. Translation was leading at first.

    . . . .

3. I'm going for a drive tomorrow.

    . . . .

4. Peter and Anne are staying at home.

    . . . .

5. Jean's having her hair done on Sunday.

    . . . .

6. Peter's going to make the beds.

    . . . .

7. Peter's made the beds. (Be careful with this one!)

    . . . .

8. That's my idea of a rest.

    . . . .

9. We're going to see Anne's folks this weekend.

    . . . .

10. Are you going to visit your friends in Boston?

    . . . .

11. My parents are going to Mexico this year.

    . . . .

12. They're going by plane.

    . . . .

EXERCISE E

Write questions for the answers.

1. .... ?
    That jockey is coaxing Homework into the starting gate. (Who)

2. .... ?
    They (the horses) are waiting for the starting signal. (What)

3. .... ?
    I'm going to Boston tomorrow. (Where)

4. .... ?
    I'm going there (to Boston) tomorrow. (When)

5. .... ?
    They (Anne's parents) are going on vacation next week. (When)

6. .... ?
    They're going to Mexico City first. (Where)

7. .... ?
    They're going to be there (in Mexico) about three weeks. (How long)

8. .... ?
    They're going by car. (How)

In the next four questions use the verb *do*.

9. .... ?
    We're going to have a rest this weekend. (What)

10. .... ?
    They (Mr. and Mrs. Parker) are going to the theater this evening. (What)

11. .... ?
    I'm not doing anything tomorrow. (What)

12. .... ?
    She (Eileen) is playing tennis with her friend this afternoon. (What)

Unit 7 □ *Text A*

Arrangements for the Visit of the Mayor of New York to a New Shopping Center in Forest Hills, Tuesday, 25th October.

The Mayor will arrive at 10 a.m.
Congressman Gross of Queens will meet the Mayor at the entrance to the shopping center.

Congressman Gross will conduct the Mayor to the platform.
There, he will meet two local political officials.
Congressman Gross will make a speech of welcome.
He will then introduce the Mayor.
The Mayor will make a brief political speech.

After the speech the Mayor will probably shake hands with members of the public.
Members of the public will be able to ask the Mayor questions.
But clearly he will not be able to talk to everyone.
At about 11:00 the Mayor will begin his tour of the shopping center.
He will visit every store.
The tour will last about half an hour.
He will meet the managers of all the stores.
In order to avoid confusion all employees will continue to work normally during the visit.
The Mayor will leave the shopping center at 11:30.

Drills

DRILL A *(6)*   □ *T: Unit 7, Drill A. Listen!* □

1. **T:** Will the Mayor arrive at 10 a.m.? *Yes.*   **S:** Yes, he will.
    T: Yes, he will.   **S:** Yes, he will.
2. **T:** Will Congressman Smith meet him?
        No.
                                                       S: No, he won't.
    T: No, he won't.   **S:** No, he won't.
       T: Now you do the same.

DRILL B *(5)*   □ *T: Unit 7, Drill B. Listen!* □

1.   **T:** Will the mayor arrive at 11 o'clock?
         No/at 10 o'clock.
                                                     S: No, he won't. He'll arrive at 10
                                                     o'clock.
     T: No, he won't. He'll arrive at 10
     o'clock.
                                                     S: No, he won't. He'll arrive at 10
                                                     o'clock.
2.   **T:** Will you be on the platform?
         No/in the audience.
                                                     S: No, I won't. I'll be in the audience.
     T: No, I won't. I'll be in the audience.   **S:** No, I won't. I'll be in the audience.
       T: Now you do the same.
     New word: Senator Jones.

DRILL C *(7)*   □ *T: Unit 7, Drill C. Listen!* □

1.   **T:** What time will the Mayor arrive?   **S:** He'll arrive at 10 a.m.
       At 10 a.m.   **S:** He'll arrive at 10 a.m.
       T: He'll arrive at 10 a.m.

2.   **T:** Who will meet him? *Congressman*
       Gross.   **S:** Congressman Gross'll meet him.
       T: Congressman Gross'll meet him.   **S:** Congressman Gross'll meet him.

3.   **T:** Where will Congressman Gross
       meet him? *At the entrance to*
       the shopping center.   **S:** He'll meet him at the entrance to the
                                                                                  shopping center.

       T: He'll meet him at the entrance to the
       shopping center.   **S:** He'll meet him at the entrance to the
                                                                                  shopping center.

       T: Now you do the same.

DRILL D *(10)*   □ *T: Unit 7, Drill D. Listen!* □

1.   **T:** The Mayor'll arrive at ten, won't he?   **S:** The Mayor'll arrive at ten, won't he?
2.   **T:** The Congressman'll meet him,
       won't he?   **S:** The Congressman'll meet him, won't
                                                                                  he?
3.   **T:** You won't be there, will you?   **S:** You won't be there, will you?
       T: Now you do the same.
New words: leave (v); chaotic.

Unit 7 □ *Text B*

THE BOSS COMES TO DINNER

PART ONE

Joan:	Oh, dear. They'll be here in a minute.
David:	No, they won't. They won't be here for at least half an hour.
Joan:	But I'll never be ready in time.
David:	Why?
Joan:	I haven't even peeled the potatoes yet.
David:	Stop worrying, Joan. I'll give you a hand.
Joan:	Oh, thanks.
David:	Where are the potatoes?
Joan:	They're in a basket in the pantry.
David:	Okay. How many shall I peel?
Joan:	Oh, a couple of dozen will be enough.
David:	That seems a lot.
Joan:	They're only small ones.
David:	All right, then.
Joan:	I'll set the table; then I'll go up and get ready.
David:	Eileen'll set the table.
Joan:	She's out. She won't be back until eight o'clock.
David:	Where's she gone?
Joan:	She's gone to the movies with some of her friends.

PART TWO

David: Mr. Hammond'll probably have his new Cadillac, and I'll have to admire it.

Joan: Yes, and his wife'll probably be wearing an expensive new dress . . .

David: I'm sure she will.

Joan: . . . and heaps of jewelry.

David: Yes, she usually wears too much.

Joan: She'll make me look absolutely shabby.

David: You'll look perfectly charming; you always do.

Joan: How sweet of you David! But you know it isn't true.

(The bell rings)

Joan: Good heavens! That's probably them now.

David: I'll go. You go upstairs and get ready.

Joan: What about the potatoes?

David: Don't worry. We'll start dinner a bit later than usual.

Joan: But what about the pota. . . .?

David: I'll do the potatoes after you come down.

(He goes to the door.)

" . . . . . AND HEAPS OF JEWELRY "

PART THREE

David:	(Calling to Joan) It's all right. It's only Eileen.
Joan:	Thank Heavens!
Eileen:	What's the matter?
Joan:	Eileen, dear, will you be an angel and peel a few potatoes?
Eileen:	Okay, Mother.
David:	Shall I set the table?
Joan:	Yes, please. You'll find the silverware on top of the cabinet in the dining room. It's all there.
David:	Oh yes. . . . I've got it.
Joan:	And don't forget the drinks, David.
David:	Don't worry. I'll give Mr. Hammond a stiff scotch as soon as they arrive. I'll have one myself too. It'll help me to be enthusiastic about his Cadillac.

"IT'LL HELP ME TO BE ENTHUSIASTIC
ABOUT HIS CADILLAC."

DRILL E *(6)*   □ *T: Unit 7, Drill E. Listen!* □

1.   **T:** Joan hasn't peeled the potatoes yet.   **S:** Joan hasn't peeled the potatoes yet.
      T: Joan hasn't peeled the potatoes yet.   **S:** Joan hasn't peeled the potatoes yet.
2.   **T:** *washed her hair.*   **S:** Joan hasn't washed her hair yet.
      T: Joan hasn't washed her hair yet.   **S:** Joan hasn't washed her hair yet.
         T: Now you do the same.
      New words: shave (n); served

DRILL F *(6)*   □ *T: Unit 7, Drill F. Listen!* □

1.   **T:** Joan's peeled the potatoes already.   **S:** Joan's peeled the potatoes already.
      T: Joan's peeled the potatoes already.   **S:** Joan's peeled the potatoes already.
2.   **T:** *washed her hair.*   **S:** Joan's washed her hair already.
      T: Joan's washed her hair already.   **S:** Joan's washed her hair already.
         T: Now you do the same.

DRILL G *(10)*   □ *T: Unit 7, Drill G. Listen and repeat.* □

1.   **T:** David told Joan to stop worrying.   **S:** David told Joan to stop worrying.
2.   **T:** David told Joan to start getting   **S:** David told Joan to start getting
         ready.   ready.
3.   **T:** Joan asked Eileen to start peeling   **S:** Joan asked Eileen to start peeling
         the potatoes.   the potatoes.
4.   **T:** The doctor told me to stop smoking.   **S:** The doctor told me to stop smoking.
5.   **T:** The doctor advised me to stop   **S:** The doctor advised me to stop
         smoking.   smoking.
6.   **T:** The doctor advised me to start   **S:** The doctor advised me to start
         doing exercises.   doing exercises.
7.   **T:** He advised Peter to stop drinking   **S:** He advised Peter to stop drinking
         so much beer.   so much beer.
8.   **T:** The last bus has gone, so we'd   **S:** The last bus has gone, so we'd
         better start walking.   better start walking.
9.   **T:** When Mr. Parker is 65, he'll stop   **S:** When Mr. Parker is 65, he'll stop
         working.   working.
10.   **T:** Mr. Parker told Bob to stop   **S:** Mr. Parker told Bob to stop
         wasting his time.   wasting his time.

DRILL H *(6)*   □ *T: Unit 7, Drill H. Listen and repeat.* □

1. **T:** Go and get ready!	**S:** Go and get ready!

2.   **T:** *You* go and get ready!
     I'll set the table.
	S: *You* go and get ready!
	     I'll set the table.

3. **T:** See who's at the door!	**S:** See who's at the door!

4.   **T:** *You* see who's at the door!
     I'm tired.
	S: *You* see who's at the door!
	     I'm tired.

5. **T:** Don't be late!	**S:** Don't be late!

6.   **T:** Don't *you* be late!
     I never *am*!
	S: Don't *you* be late!
	     I never *am*!

DRILL I *(5)*   □ *Unit 7, Drill I. Listen!* □

1.   **T:** Don't forget the drinks!
     T: You won't forget the drinks, will
        you?
	S: You won't forget the drinks, will you?
	
	S: You won't forget the drinks, will you?

2.   **T:** Don't work too hard!
     T: You won't work too hard, will you?
     T: Now you do the same.
	S: You won't work too hard, will you?
	S: You won't work too hard, will you?

ORAL AND WRITTEN EXERCISES

EXERCISE A

Make questions from these sentences, beginning with the words in parentheses.

1.   The Mayor will arrive at 10 o'clock. (What time)

. . . .

2.   Congressman Gross will meet him at the entrance to the shopping center. (Where)

. . . .

3.   The Congressman will conduct him to the platform. (Who)

. . . .

4.   Two political officials will meet the Mayor there. (How many)

. . . .

5.   Congressman Gross will make a speech of welcome. (Who)

. . . .

6.   The Mayor will make a brief political speech. (Will)

. . . .

7.   Members of the public will be able to ask the Mayor questions. (What — use the verb *do*)

. . . .

8.   He will visit every store in the shopping center. (Which)

. . . .

9.   The tour will take about half an hour. (How long)

. . . .

10.   He will meet the managers of the stores. (Who)

. . . .

EXERCISE B

Answer these questions as in the example:

Q: Will he arrive at ten thirty? (No/at ten)

A: *No, he won't. He'll arrive at ten.*

1.   Will you make a speech? (No/the Congressman)

    ....

2.   Will the President be there? (No/the Mayor)

    ....

3.   Will Joan set the table? (No/David)

    ....

4.   Will the potatoes be in the garage? (No/in the pantry)

    ....

5.   Will Eileen set the table? (No/David)

    ....

6.   Will Joan look shabby? (No/charming)

    ....

7.   Will Mrs. Hammond be wearing a cheap dress? (No/an expensive one)

    ....

8.   Will Mr. Hammond be driving his old car? (No/his new Cadillac)

    ....

9.   Will they have dinner at the usual time? (No/a bit later than usual)

    ....

10.   Will David find the silverware in the kitchen? (No/in the dining room)

    ....

EXERCISE C

Rephrase these sentences as in the example:

Open the window.

Will you open the window, please?

1. Peel the potatoes.

    . . . .

2. Go and get ready.

    . . . .

3. Wait a minute.

    . . . .

4. Set the table.

    . . . .

5. Answer the door.

    . . . .

6. Get me a stiff scotch.

    . . . .

7. Tell me the answer.

    . . . .

8. Help me do this exercise.

    . . . .

9. Learn this conversation.

    . . . .

10. Show me how this machine works.

    . . . .

EXERCISE D

Rephrase these questions as in the example:

Do you want me to open the window?

Shall I open the window?

1. Do you want me to set the table?

. . . .

2. Do you want me to peel the potatoes?

. . . .

3. Do you want me to answer the door?

. . . .

4. Do you want me to offer them a drink?

. . . .

5. Do you want me to wear my new dress?

. . . .

6. Do you want me to show you the way to the station?

. . . .

7. Do you want me to go with you to the stores?

. . . .

8. Do you want me to meet you in town?

. . . .

9. Do you want me to buy some cigarettes?

. . . .

10. Do you want me to write to you?

. . . .

EXERCISE E

Construct sentences from the elements provided, as in the example:

Mrs. Hammond/Joan Parker/look absolutely shabby.

Mrs. Hammond made Joan Parker look absolutely shabby.

1.   The teacher/student/do the exercise again.

. . . .

2.   Anne/Peter/promise to come home early.

. . . .

3.   The policeman/the thief/empty his pockets.

. . . .

4.   Anne/Bill/put his toys away.

. . . .

5.   You/me/miss my train.

. . . .

EXERCISE F

Rephrase these sentences, as in the example:

They took an hour to repair the radio.

It took them an hour to repair the radio.

1.   Joan took a long time to get ready.

. . . .

2.   David took ten minutes to set the table.

. . . .

3.   We took ten minutes to do the exercise.

. . . .

4.   They took six hours to get to Boston by train.

. . . .

5.   Some people take longer than others to learn a language.

. . . .

Unit 8 □ *Text A*

ANNE'S VISIT

PART ONE:

Joan Parker:	You're all going to be in tonight, aren't you?
David Parker:	Oh yes, Anne's coming over, isn't she?
Joan:	Yes. *You* aren't going out, are you, Eileen?
Eileen:	No. But what about Bob?
Bob:	Well, as a matter of fact, . . .
Eileen:	. . . you won't be *in*, will you?
Bob:	. . . as a matter of fact . . .
Eileen:	. . . you'll be taking *Georgia* out, won't you?
Bob:	. . . as a matter of fact, I'm *not* going out this evening.
Eileen:	Good heavens! Wonders will never cease!

PART TWO

Joan Parker:	Well, your vacation *was* a success, wasn't it?
Anne:	It certainly *was*.
Joan Parker:	You didn't bring any photographs to show us, did you?
Anne:	Of course! I almost forgot. They're in my handbag.
Joan Parker:	You left it in the dining room, didn't you?
Anne:	It's here, on the floor. . . . Here they are.
Joan Parker:	Oh yes! This was taken near the motel, wasn't it?
Anne:	That's right.
Joan Parker:	Look David. The children look very well, don't they?
David Parker:	They certainly *do*. Bill's grown a lot, hasn't he?
Joan Parker:	Well you haven't seen him for ages, have you?
David Parker:	No, not for three or four months.
Joan Parker:	This is a nice one of Anne and Eileen, isn't it?
David Parker:	Yes. There aren't many of Peter, are there?
Anne:	Well, he took most of them, you see.
David Parker:	There weren't a lot of motels near you, were there?
Anne:	No; just two or three about half a mile away.

David Parker:	Very nice. But not quite perfect.
Anne:	What do you mean?
David Parker:	Well! There wasn't a golf course for miles, was there!

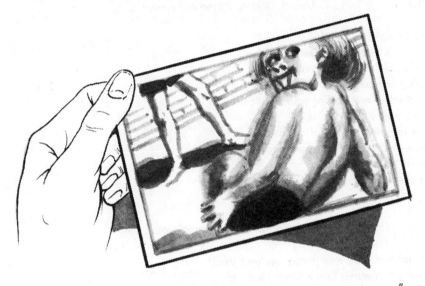

"BILL'S GROWN A LOT, HASN'T HE?"

"THIS IS A NICE ONE OF ANNE AND EILEEN, ISN'T IT?"

Drills

DRILL A *(10)*   □ *T: Unit 8, Drill A. Listen and repeat.* □

1.   T: It's a lovely day, isn't it?
2.   T: Anne's coming tonight, isn't she?
3.   T: You're staying home, aren't you?
4.   T: Bob's going out, isn't he?
5.   T: The children are looking well, aren't they?
6.   T: It isn't a very nice day, is it?
7.   T: Anne isn't coming tomorrow, is she?
8.   T: You aren't staying home, are you?
9.   T: Bob isn't going out, is he?
10. T: The children aren't looking well, are they?

DRILL B *(10)*   □ *T: Unit 8, Drill B. Listen and repeat.* □

1.   T: The children were very happy, weren't they?
2.   T: The children weren't very happy, were they?
3.   T: The weather was excellent, wasn't it?
4.   T: The weather wasn't very good, was it?
5.   T: Bob was in when Anne came, wasn't he?
6.   T: He wasn't out when Anne came, was he?
7.   T: Eileen hasn't been to Florida, has she?
8.   T: She's been to Maine, hasn't she?
9.   T: You'll help me with my work, won't you?
10. T: You won't forget to write to me, will you?

DRILL C *(10)*   □ *T: Unit 8, Drill C. Listen and repeat.* □

1.   **T:** Mr. Parker works in a department store, doesn't he?
2.   **T:** Miss Jones comes from New York, doesn't she?
3.   **T:** The Parkers live in a house, don't they?
4.   **T:** Mr. Gordon doesn't teach at a college, does he?
5.   **T:** You don't come from Mexico, do you?
6.   **T:** Hans and Lotte visited the Parkers, didn't they?
7.   **T:** They went to Elmhurst by train, didn't they?
8.   **T:** Joan asked her guests what they would like to drink, didn't she?
9.   **T:** David drove his guests to the center of town, didn't he?
10. **T:** He didn't take any photographs, did he?

DRILL D *(10)*   □ *T: Unit 8, Drill D. Listen and repeat.* □

1.   **T:** There's a big store on the corner, isn't there?
2.   **T:** There aren't any stores on this street, are there?
3.   **T:** There are some children on the beach, aren't there?
4.   **T:** There aren't any children near the river, are there?
5.   **T:** There were a lot of cars on the road, weren't there?
6.   **T:** There weren't so many cars in Maine, were there?
7.   **T:** There was plenty of room on the beach, wasn't there?
8.   **T:** There's been an air crash in California, hasn't there?
9.   **T:** There've been a lot of crashes this year, haven't there?
10. **T:** There'll be a holiday on Election Day, won't there?

Unit 8 □ *Text B*

LAST-MINUTE INSTRUCTIONS

PART ONE

Joan:	Oh Bob, I have to go shopping this morning.
Bob:	What time will you be back?
Joan:	About twelve-thirty.
Bob:	That means one o'clock, then!
Joan:	I have to go to five different stores.
Bob:	But that won't take two and a half hours, will it?
Joan:	Yes. They're always terribly busy on Saturday mornings.
Bob:	Why do you always choose Saturdays to go shopping?
Joan:	I don't. I usually go downtown on Fridays.
Bob:	You went last Saturday.
Eileen:	Oh be quiet, Bob. You're always arguing.
Bob:	I never argue. I merely state facts.

"THEY'RE ALWAYS TERRIBLY BUSY ON SATURDAY MORNINGS"

PART TWO

Eileen:	If the milkman comes, shall I get anything?
Joan:	Oh yes. If he comes, get three pints of milk and a pound of whipped butter.
Eileen:	What about cream?
Joan:	A half a pint of half and half.
Eileen:	Shall I pay him?
Joan:	No. Tell him I'll pay him when he comes on Tuesday.
Eileen:	What about the cleaners? What shall I give him if he comes?
Joan:	I've left two suits in the front hall.
Eileen:	What about lunch?
Joan:	I've gotten everything ready.
Eileen:	Have you set the timer?
Joan:	Yes. As soon as you hear the buzzer, put the vegetables on.
Eileen:	How long shall I let them boil?
Joan:	Just until they're cooked. Then you can turn the burner off.
Eileen:	What about the meat?
Joan:	Don't worry about the meat. I'll take care of that when I get back.

"JUST UNTIL THEY'RE COOKED"

PART THREE

Bob: Anne sometimes calls on Saturday morning, doesn't she?
Joan: Yes, she does.
Bob: What shall I say if she calls while you're out?
Joan: Good heavens! You're her brother, aren't you? Just talk to her.
Bob: Talk? I can't just *talk*.
Joan: Let Eileen answer the phone, then. She usually does, anyway.
Bob: It's all right. I'll answer it if it rings.
Eileen: Ah-ha! So you're expecting a call from Georgia, are you? I see.
Bob: Clever, aren't you!
Joan: I'll have to go now. You won't forget what I've told you, will you, Eileen?
Eileen: No. I'll remember everything.
Bob: You'll have to hurry, or you won't be home in time for lunch.
Joan: Goodbye.
Eileen: }
Bob: } Goodbye.

"SO YOU'RE EXPECTING A CALL FROM GEORGIA, ARE YOU?"

DRILL E *(8)*   ☐ *T: Unit 8, Drill E. Listen!* ☐

1. **T:** I have to go shopping this
        afternoon.   **S:** I have to go shopping this afternoon.
    T: I have to go shopping this
        afternoon.   **S:** I have to go shopping this afternoon.
2. **T:** *do some work this afternoon.*   **S:** I have to do some work this afternoon.
    T: I have to do some work this
        afternoon.   **S:** I have to do some work this afternoon.
    T: Now you do the same.

DRILL F *(7)*   ☐ *T: Unit 8, Drill F. Listen!* ☐

1. **T:** If John calls, I'll talk to him.   **S:** If John calls, I'll talk to him.
    T: If John calls, I'll talk to him.   **S:** If John calls, I'll talk to him.
2. **T:** *When*   **S:** When John calls, I'll talk to him.
    T: When John calls, I'll talk to him.   **S:** When John calls, I'll talk to him.
    T: Now you do the same.

DRILL G *(10)*   ☐ *T: Unit 8, Drill G. Listen and repeat.* ☐

1. **T:** When I've read this book, I'll give it to you.
2. **T:** As soon as I've read this book, I'll give it to you.
3. **T:** After I've read this book, I'll give it to you.
4. **T:** When she's finished her work, she'll write to Anne.
5. **T:** After she's finished her work, she'll write to Anne.
6. **T:** He can't talk to you before he's taken this exam.
7. **T:** He can't talk to you until he's taken this exam.
8. **T:** What will you do when they've gone?
9. **T:** What will you do after they've gone.
10. **T:** What shall we do before they arrive.

ORAL AND WRITTEN EXERCISES

EXERCISE A

Complete the following questions as in the examples:

They won't be late, ... they?

They won't be late, *will* . . . they?

They'll be late, ... they?

They'll be late, *won't* . they?

1.   This is your hat, ... it?

2.   This isn't your hat, ... it?

3.   There's a bar on the corner, ... there?

4.   There isn't a bar on the corner, ... there?

5.   John's staying with you next week, ... ?

6.   John isn't staying with you next week, ... ?

7.   John's decided to become a doctor, ... ?

8.   You're going for a drive tomorrow, ... ?

9.   You were rather tired last night, ... ?

10.   There weren't many people at the concert, ... ?

11.   There were quite a lot of people at the concert, ... ?

12.   There've been a lot of accidents this week, ... ?

13.   You'll stay for dinner, ... ?

14.   There'll be four people in the car, ... ?

15.   There'll be trouble if she arrives home after midnight, ... ?

16.   I'm the last on the list, ... ?

17.   He understood what I told him, ... ?

18.   You understand this question, ... ?

19.   He doesn't understand Russian, ... ?

20.   You don't understand this question, ... ?

21.   She listened to the news this evening, ... ?

22.   She listens to the news every evening, ... ?

EXERCISE B

PART ONE

Compare these two sentences:
  (a)   She's going shopping this morning.
  (b)   She has to go shopping this morning.
  Rewrite the following using *have to*, etc. as in (b)

1.   She's going downtown this morning.

. . . .

2.   Joan's going to five different stores.

. . . .

3.   You're visiting your mother today, aren't you?

. . . .

4.   I'm going now.

. . . .

5.   Bob got up early this morning, didn't he?

. . . .

6.   Eileen put the vegetables on, didn't she?

. . . .

PART TWO

Note: Instead of *have to,* many people say *have got to* (e.g. She's got to go shopping this
      morning.)
      Rewrite sentences 1–6 using *have got to*

1.   . . . .

2.   . . . .

3.   . . . .

4.   . . . .

5.   . . . .

6.   . . . .

PART THREE

Note: In the interrogative and negative forms, the construction *have to* is always used
(e.g. Does she have to go shopping this morning?)
Rewrite sentences 1—6 (a) in the negative and (b) in the interrogative, using *have to.*

1. (a) ....

   (b) ....

2. (a) ....

   (b) ....

3. (a) ....

   (b) ....

4. (a) ....

   (b) ....

5. (a) ....

   (b) ....

6. (a) ....

   (b) ....

EXERCISE C

After each of the following incomplete sentences you will see a list of four words. Of these one or more can be used to complete the sentence. *Underline the word or words which could be used to complete each sentence.*

1. He looks . . . . tired.
    pretty / quite / well / enough

2. This track is shorter than the . . . . one.
    normal /usual / usually / ordinary

3. I saw the race . . . . television.
    in / on / off / from

4. I'm staying . . . . home this weekend.
    in / by / to / at

5. Who'll take care . . . . the children while you're away?
    after / at / of / with

6. We're going . . . . vacation next week.
    to / on / off / at

7. Are you going . . . . car?
    in / on / by / with

8. The horse is . . . . signs of tiring.
    indicating / demonstrating / showing / making

9. Lazy Student is . . . . to win.
    sure / probable / bound / certain

10. Your car has four doors, ... it?
    is / isn't / doesn't / don't

EXERCISE D

Rewrite these sentences, inserting the adverbs given in brackets. (Note that many adverbs are not restricted to one position in a sentence. Ask your teacher about the options.)

1. (always) He speaks English when he has the chance.

. . . .

2. (very well) He speaks English.

. . . .

3. (generally) I have a cup of coffee after dinner.

. . . .

4. (certainly) He will help you if he can.

. . . .

5. (never) He arrives at the office on time.

. . . .

6. (badly) He needs a haircut.

. . . .

7. (badly) They all answered the first question.

. . . .

8. (often) These students work until midnight.

. . . .

9. (sometimes) I go fishing on Sundays.

. . . .

10. (too quickly) The boy is eating the candy I gave him.

. . . .

11. (ever) Have you been to New Orleans?

. . . .

12. (always) Does he go to work by train?

. . . .

13. (usually) I'm too tired to work in the evening.

. . . .

14.   (very often) He has a nap on Sunday afternoons.

. . . .

15.   (very fast) Bob drives his father's car.

. . . .

16.   (very much) I like Paris.

. . . .

17.   (very much) I hope you will be able to come.

. . . .

18.   (always) The stores are terribly busy on Saturdays.

. . . .

19.   (always) Are the stores busy on Saturdays?

. . . .

20.   (always) She chooses Saturday to go shopping.

. . . .

21.   (always) Why does she choose Saturday to go shopping?

. . . .

22.   (usually) I go downtown on Fridays.

. . . .

23.   (never) I argue.

. . . .

24.   (sometimes) Anne calls on Saturday morning.

. . . .

EXERCISE E

Complete these sentences with words used in Units 7 & 8:

1.   He met the Mayor at the . . . . to the shopping center.

2.   The Mayor made a . . . . political . . . .

3.   The Mayor will . . . . shake hands with members of the public.

4.   Everyone continued to work . . . . during the visit.

5.   At about 11:00 the Mayor . . . . his tour of the shopping center.

6.   I'll never be ready . . . . time.

7.   David offered to give his wife a . . . .

8.   The potatoes are in the . . . .

9.   Who'll . . . . the table?

10. The boss will . . . . come in his new Cadillac.

11. His wife was . . . . too much jewelry.

12. David thought Joan looked perfectly . . . .

13. You'll find the . . . . on the top of the cabinet in the dining room.

14. It was hard for David to be . . . . about his boss's new car.

15. Aren't you ready . . . . ?

16. Anne's coming . . . . tonight.

17. As a . . . . of fact, I'm *not* going out.

18. . . . . will never cease!

19. Peter looks well, doesn't he. He certainly . . . .

20. The photographs were in Anne's . . . .

21. The stores are . . . . busy on Saturday mornings.

22. Why do you always . . . . Saturdays to go shopping?

23. Be quiet! You're always . . . .

24. Peter isn't in many of the photographs because he . . . . most of them.

Unit 9 □ *Text A*
ANIMAL, VEGETABLE OR MINERAL

PART ONE

Master of Ceremonies:	Good evening, ladies and gentlemen. Welcome to our weekly game of "Animal, Vegetable or Mineral." Let me introduce the panel. First, Sheila Andrews.
SA:	Good evening.
MC:	Elizabeth Mills.
EM:	Hello.
MC:	Monty Hughes.
MH:	Hi.
MC:	And last but not least — Ted Forbes.
TF:	Good evening.
MC:	Okay. Now you all know the rules, don't you? The first object is mainly mineral, but it contains some vegetable.
EM:	Can you eat it?
MC:	No, you can't.
SA:	Can you drink it?
MC:	No, you can't.
MH:	Can you wear it?
MC:	No.
TF:	Can you smell it?
MC:	No.
MH:	Can you buy these things in a store?
MC:	You're assuming too much. I can't answer that question with a Yes or No.
EM:	Now I wonder what's wrong with that question! Oh . . . Is this thing unique?
MC:	Yes.
EM:	Could I own it?
MC:	No.
EM:	Could I lift it?
MC:	No.
EM:	Could anyone lift it?
MC:	No.
TF:	Is it a place?
MC:	Well . . . yes.
TF:	I wonder why he hesitated. Is it a building?
MC:	Yes, it is.

114

SA:	If I visited this building, would I be allowed in?
MC:	Yes.
SA:	Could I go in without paying?
MC:	No.
SA:	Is it a museum?
MC:	No, it isn't.
MH:	If I went to London could I visit it?
MC:	No, you couldn't.
MH:	If I went to Paris, could I visit it?
MC:	Yes, you could.
TF:	Can you buy postcards of this building?
MC:	Yes, you can.
EM:	Is it very tall?
MC:	Yes, it is.
EM:	It's the Eiffel Tower.
MC:	Yes. That's right. But you were all very slow, weren't you?

PART TWO

MC:	The next object could be animal, vegetable to mineral.
TF:	May I ask a preliminary question?
MC:	You may certainly ask a preliminary question, but I may not answer it!
TF:	Could this object be a mixture of substances?
MC:	I thought you might ask that question. Yes, it could.
TF:	So it isn't a unique object this time?
MC:	No. There are millions of them.
TF:	Might I own one?
MC:	Yes, you might. You probably do, in fact.
SA:	Would I carry it around with me?
MC:	Well, you might. People might think you were a bit eccentric if you did, though.
MH:	Do you have one of these things?
MC:	Yes, I have lots of them.
EM:	Do these things occur in a natural state, or do people make them?
MC:	Which part of the question do you want me to answer?
EM:	Do people make them?
MC:	Yes, they do.
EM:	Might I make one?
MC:	You might.
EM:	If I made one, would I eat it?
MC:	No, you wouldn't eat it. Look! I'm going to help you: You wouldn't eat it, you wouldn't drink it and you wouldn't wear it.
EM:	What a kind Master of Ceremonies you are! Would I use it in the house?
MC:	Yes.
EM:	Would I sit on it?
MC:	You might; but you'd probably regret it if you did. You certainly wouldn't sit on it deliberately.
TF:	It isn't a piece of furniture, then?
MC:	Not in the usual sense.
TF:	Would I find it in the kitchen?
MC:	You might. In fact, you might find it in *any* room of the house.
SA:	Is it a receptacle of some kind?
MC:	Yes, you might call it that.
SA:	So if I had one, I might keep things in it?
MC:	Not exactly. You might *put* things in it, but you wouldn't *keep* them there.
TF:	Is this receptacle for a particular kind of thing?
MC:	Yes.
TF:	For jewelry?
MC:	Far from it!

EM:	It's for garbage then?
MC:	More or less.
EM:	It's a garbage can.
MC:	Wrong.

SA:	It's a wastepaper basket.
MC:	Wrong again!

EM:	I know! It's an ash tray.
MC:	Correct.

MH:	Wait a moment. I object!
MC:	Why?
MH:	How can an ash tray be vegetable?
MC:	It could be made of wood, couldn't it?
MH:	So it could! But it certainly couldn't be animal.
MC:	Why not? Haven't you ever seen an ivory ash tray, or a horn ash tray, or a shell ash tray . . .?
MH:	Oh, you win!

Drills

DRILL A *(6)*   □ *T: Unit 9, Drill A. Listen!* □

1. T: Can you speak French? *Yes.*   S: Yes, I can.
    T: Yes, I can.   S: Yes, I can.
2. T: Can Eileen speak French? *No.*   S: No, she can't.
    T: No, she can't.   S: No, she can't.
        T: Now you do the same.
    New words: basketball; bicycle.

DRILL B *(6)*   □ *T: Unit 9, Drill B. Listen!* □

1. T: If you went to Paris, could you
        see the Eiffel Tower? *Yes.*   S: Yes, you could.
    T: Yes, you could.   S: Yes, you could.
2. T: Could you see the Empire State
        Building? *No.*   S: No, you couldn't.
    T: No, you couldn't.   S: No, you couldn't.
        T: Now you do the same.
    New words: Golden Gate Bridge; Central Park; Empire State Building; the Seine;
        Napoleon's tomb.

DRILL C *(6)*   □ *T: Unit 9, Drill C. Listen!* □

1. T: If I lent you this book, would
        you read it? *Yes.*   S: Yes, I would.
    T: Yes, I would.   S: Yes, I would.
2. T: If I lent Eileen this book, would
        she read it? *No.*   S: No, she wouldn't.
    T: No, she wouldn't.   S: No, she wouldn't.
    T: Now you do the same.
    New words: lent (past tense of *lend*); Governor; Times Square

Unit 9 □ *Text B*

A LAZY SATURDAY AFTERNOON

PART ONE

JP: David, we shouldn't sit here doing nothing.
DP: Why not? It's Saturday afternoon, isn't it?
JP: Yes, but there's so much to do around the house.
DP: It can wait.
JP: We ought to finish washing down the kitchen walls and cupboards.
DP: We can do that tomorrow. We don't have to do it today.
JP: All right. But we must do it tomorrow, because the painters are coming on Monday.
DP: Yes. And that reminds me. I must do something about that leak under the kitchen sink.
JP: That's a good idea.
DP: Talking about washing down the kitchen — where's Bob?

"IT CAN WAIT"

JP: He's having lunch with Georgia.
DP: What! Again?
JP: He should be in soon.
DP: He shouldn't spend so much time with that girl.
JP: You must be patient, David. Nineteen's a very difficult age, you know.
DP: Yes, I know. But he ought to be studying more.

". . . HE OUGHT TO BE STUDYING MORE"

PART TWO

DP: By the way, would you like to go to the movies this evening?

JP: I'd love to. But I *must* write some letters.

DP: Why tonight?

JP: I haven't written to anyone for ages. Sylvia and John must think I've forgotten them.

DP: You don't have to write. You can call them tomorrow. It's half-price on Sundays.

JP: Yes I could, couldn't I? All right. I'll do that. What's playing then?

DP: Let's see. Here we are. 'The RKO Columbia: *Blood in the Bathtub*. A must for all teenagers.'

JP: No thank you!

DP: 'The Central. *Scandal in Scandinavia*. All parents of teenage children ought to see this picture.'

JP: What about the Rex?

DP: Oh God. It's that awful child prodigy . . .

JP: There *must* be something worth seeing somewhere.

DP: What about this. 'John Wayne in: *Texas, Here I Come.*'

JP: I can't stand Westerns.

DP: Neither can I. Listen Joan. I've got a better idea.

DP: }
JP: } (together) Let's stay at home and wash down the kitchen walls!

" I'VE GOT A BETTER IDEA "

ORAL AND WRITTEN EXERCISES

EXERCISE A

Underline the word or words which could be used to complete each sentence:

1. I . . . . go and see the doctor tomorrow.
   must / should / ought

2. You . . . . to read these instructions first.
   must / should / ought

3. He should be in soon, ... he?
   didn't / shouldn't / hadn't

4. If you went to Agra, you . . . . see the Taj Mahal.
   can / could

5. If I had a knife, I . . . . cut this string.
   can / could

6. If I had a flashlight, I . . . . carry it around with me.
   wouldn't / won't

7. We . . . . watch the Kentucky Derby on television yesterday afternoon.
   could / were able to

8. We . . . . watch the Kentucky Derby on television tomorrow.
   could / can / might / were able to

9. We'll . . . . watch the Kentucky Derby tomorrow.
   can / may / be able to / ought to

10. I'll . . . . write some letters this evening.
    must / have to / can / don't have to

11. They'd help you if they . . . .
    would / should / can / could

12. I'll help you if I . . . .
    would / should / can / could

EXERCISE B

Complete these sentences as in the examples:
Examples:

(a)   They won't be late, ... they?   (b)   They'll be late, ... ?

They won't be late, *will* they?   They'll be late, *won't they.* ?

1.   We can go now, ... we?

2.   They can't go yet, ... ?

3.   You can't eat it, ... ?

4.   We could go there together, ... ?

5.   They went there together, ... ?

6.   They've gone there together, ... ?

7.   It's broken, ... ?

8.   He's broken it, ... ?

9.   He can come in now, ... ?

10.   He might arrive before Wednesday, ... ?

11.   This object isn't unique, ... ?

12.   He thought I'd made a mistake, ... ?

13.   If I made one of these things, I wouldn't eat it, ... ?

14.   He'd be sorry if he ate it, ... ?

15.   We don't have to write the whole sentence, ... ?

16.   We could go to Canada tomorrow, ... ?

17.   An ash tray could be made of wood, ... ?

18.   He managed to get some tickets for the concert, ... ?

19. You want to get up early tomorrow, ...?

20. The master of ceremonies doesn't have to answer every question, ...?

21. They shouldn't work so hard, ...?

22. We should wash down the kitchen walls, ...?

23. She doesn't have to write a letter, ...?

24. She wouldn't like to go to the movies, ...?

EXERCISE C

Here is another game of *Animal, Vegetable or Mineral.* Provide suitable questions in the spaces provided. Use questions containing *or* in those marked like this: *Q

Master of Ceremonies: The next object is mineral.

1. Q: . . . .
    MC: No, it isn't unique.

2. Q: . . . .
    MC: Yes, there are millions and millions of them.

3. Q: . . . .
    MC: No, they don't exist in one country only. There are plenty in every country.

4. Q: . . . .
    MC: No, they aren't found in their natural state; they're manufactured.

5. Q: . . . .
    MC: Yes, I do. In fact, I have three.

6. Q: . . . .
    MC: Yes, I'm sure you do.

7. Q: . . . .
    MC: No, it's very light.

8. Q: . . . .

    MC: Yes, I generally carry one around with me.

9. *Q: . . . .

    MC: Some are cheap; others are expensive.

10. Q: . . . .

    MC: No, it isn't a cigarette lighter.

11. Q: . . . .

    MC: It's a *very* useful object!

12. Q: . . . .

    MC: Oh yes! I could certainly live without it!

13. *Q: . . . .

    MC: I carry mine around in my *coat* pocket — never in my *trouser* pocket.

14. Q: . . . .

    MC: Yes, I think most women have one of these objects.

15. Q: . . . .

    MC: No, it isn't a pencil.

16. Q: . . . .

    MC: Yes, it's a pen . . . but it's a special *kind* of pen.

17. Q: . . . .

    MC: No, it isn't a fountain pen. I'll give you one more chance.

18. Q: . . . .

    MC: Yes! It's a . . . . pen!

Unit 10 □ *Text A*

AN INTERNATIONAL EXHIBITION

An International Exhibition of business machines and industrial equipment was formally opened this morning by the Governor of California.

This exhibition has been organized by the National Association of Manufacturers.

The Governor was asked if he would like to operate one or two of the machines. Considerable amusement was caused when he hesitated, since the machines in question were fully automated, and all that he was required to do was to press a button.

CONSIDERABLE AMUSEMENT WAS CAUSED WHEN HE HESITATED

About forty per cent of all the machines exhibited are operated in this way.

A large part of the exhibition is, in fact, devoted to automation.

The exhibition is not intended, according to the organizers, to benefit only American industry.

It is hoped that all countries participating in the exhibition will benefit equally from the publicity given to their machines and equipment.

We are informed by the organizers that orders have already been placed for a wide range of machines and manufactured goods.

It is expected that the exhibition will be visited by more than a million people.

125

Drills

DRILL A *(5)*   □ *T: Unit 10, Drill A. Listen!* □

1.   **T:** The Governor was asked to open
         the Exhibition.
                                        S: The Governor was asked to open the
                                              Exhibition.

     T: The Governor was asked to open
         the Exhibition
                                        S: The Governor was asked to open the
                                              Exhibition.

2.   **T:** *expected.*   **S:** The Governor was expected to open the
                                              Exhibition.

     T: The Governor was expected to
         open the Exhibition.
                                        S: The Governor was expected
                                              to open the Exhibition.

     T: Now you do the same.

DRILL B *(7)*   □ *T: Unit 10, Drill B. Listen!* □

1.   **T:** It's expected that the
         Governor will open the
         Exhibition.
                                        S: It's expected that the Governor will
                                              open the Exhibition.

     T: It's expected that the
         Governor will open the
         Exhibition.
                                        S: It's expected that the Governor will
                                              open the Exhibition.

2.   **T:** *hoped.*   **S:** It's hoped that the Governor will open
                                              the Exhibition.

     T: It's hoped that the Governor
         will open the Exhibition.
                                        S: It's hoped that the Governor will open
                                              the Exhibition.

     T: Now you do the same.
New words: believed; assumed

Unit 10 □ *Text B*

NOTE ON TEXT B: TALKING ABOUT INCOME TAX

The Texts of all the earlier recorded conversations in this course have been reproduced in their written form.

This text, however, is given *only* on the tape.

The conversation is recorded first from beginning to end without interruption and then in two parts.

Listen to the complete conversation, and do Drill C. (See below). When you have done the drill, listen to Part One of the conversation again. (This follows the drill on the tape). At the end of Part One, stop the tape. Then answer the printed questions on page 135. If you have difficulty in answering the questions, rewind the tape and listen to Part One again.

Then do the same with Part Two.

The two speakers are Peter Wood and his friend, Bill Porter.

"THE ARMED FORCES HAVE BEEN GIVEN A BIG PAY RAISE....."

"PERSONAL INCOME TAX OUGHT TO BE REDUCED........"

DRILL C *(24)*   □ *Unit 10, Drill C. Listen and repeat.* □

1.   **T:** Personal income tax ought to be reduced.
2.   **T:** I doubt whether it will be reduced.
3.   **T:** It was reduced in the last tax appropriations bill.
4.   **T:** It won't be reduced in the pending tax bill.
5.   **T:** Government workers have been given a big pay raise.
6.   **T:** The Armed Forces have also been given a big pay raise.
7.   **T:** More money will have to be found for all that.
8.   **T:** The money could be found in other ways.
9.   **T:** The wheat subsidy could be lifted.
10.   **T:** The tax on capital gains could be increased.
11.   **T:** They could do away with some tax write-offs for depreciation.
12.   **T:** Peter thinks they should also reduce welfare payments.
13.   **T:** He also thinks that they should reduce the amount of Federal money spent on urban renewal and poverty programs.
14.   **T:** Where does he think the money for these programs should come from?
15.   **T:** He thinks it should be raised by the individual States.
16.   **T:** Would they be affected by a reduction in Federal funds?
17.   **T:** No, they wouldn't.
18.   **T:** But a great many states would be badly hit if they lost their Federal subsidies for these programs.
19.   **T:** How do *you* think the money should be found?
20.   **T:** Expense accounts should be taxed.
21.   **T:** That's nonsense!
22.   **T:** Buyers have to be taken out to lunch and dinner.
23.   **T:** People have to be entertained in business.
24.   **T:** It's often the best way to clinch an important deal.

"IT'S OFTEN THE BEST WAY TO CLINCH AN IMPORTANT DEAL."

Unit 10 □ *Text C*

A LOVERS' QUARREL

Scene: Georgia's house

PART ONE

The telephone rings.

Georgia (picking up the telephone): Hello! Is that you Kenneth?

Bob: Hello! Is that you, Georgia?

Georgia: Yes, Kenneth. I was wondering whether you'd call this evening.

Bob: Listen, Georgia. This is Bob, not Kenneth. Who on earth is Kenneth, anyway?

Georgia: Oh! It's *you*, Bob. I'm sorry. I was expecting a call from somebody else.

Bob: I've been trying to get you since two o'clock.

Georgia: Have you? I've been out. I only came in half an hour ago.

Bob: Where've you been?

Georgia: I've been playing tennis at the club.

Bob: You told me you weren't going to play tennis today.

Georgia: Yes, I know. But Madge asked me to make up a foursome.

Bob: Oh! That's really something!

PART TWO

Bob: What's the matter, Georgia? You seem to have been avoiding me lately.

Georgia: Avoiding you? Of course I haven't been avoiding you. We went out on Wednesday, didn't we?

Bob: Yes, but that's three days ago. Georgia! I want to see you very much. Can we go out tonight?

Georgia: Oh, not tonight, Bob. I'm feeling a bit tired.

Bob: Couldn't we go out for just an hour? I've been looking forward to seeing you all day.

Georgia: I can see you haven't been playing tennis all day or you . . .

Bob: I wish I had. I've been helping my old man wash the car and mow the lawn.

Georgia: Then *you* must be feeling tired too!

Bob: Listen darling? Are you telling me the truth? Or are you going out with this Kenneth, whoever he is?

Georgia: Of course not. He's . . .

Bob: You're going out with him tonight, aren't you?

Georgia: No, I've told you. I don't want to go out tonight.

Bob: Now I know why. You're going to sit by the phone all evening, waiting for your beloved Kenny to telephone.

Georgia: Don't be ridiculous, Bob. He isn't my beloved Kenny. And anyway . . . his name is Kenneth. He doesn't like to be called Kenny.

PART THREE

Bob: Oh! He doesn't, doesn't he? Well, if I get my hands on him, he won't know what's hit him. I suppose you've been seeing this poor slob every day. That's why you haven't had time for me.

Georgia: Of course it isn't. Do stop talking nonsense, Bob, and listen . . .

Bob: To your explanation? Don't bother. I understand everything now. (He imitates her) 'Oh, hello, Kenneth darling. I was wondering whether you'd call tonight.' I'm not a fool you know.

Georgia: For the last time . . . will you listen?

Bob: Go on. I'm all ears.

Georgia: Kenneth is my cousin. He's thirty-four, married and has three children. He's coming to New York next week from Colorado and he'll be staying with us. We're expecting a call from him tonight.

Bob: Your cousin? Honestly? Married? Why on earth didn't you say so?

Georgia: You didn't give me the chance.

Bob: When can I see you again?

Georgia: I'll be ready in half an hour . . . unless you're feeling too ashamed of yourself.

Bob: Me? Ashamed of myself? What for?

DRILL D

1. T: I was wondering whether you'd call this evening.
2. T: I was expecting a call from somebody else.
3. T: Georgia was expecting a call from her cousin.
4. T: She's been playing tennis.
5. T: Bob's been trying to get Georgia on the phone.
6. T: He thinks she's been avoiding him.
7. T: She says she hasn't been avoiding him.
8. T: Bob's been looking forward to seeing Georgia all day.
9. T: He's been helping his father mow the lawn.
10. T: He hasn't been playing tennis.

Now listen to Text C again and repeat the words of both speakers in the pauses provided.

ORAL AND WRITTEN EXERCISES

EXERCISE A

Complete these statements by giving the correct form of the verbs provided in the parentheses:

1. The Exhibition was . . . . by the Governor. (open)

2. The Exhibition was first . . . . by the National Association of Manufacturers. (propose)

3. The distinguished visitors were . . . . around the Exhibition by the Chairman. (show)

4. They were . . . . by the great variety of exhibits. (impress)

5. I am . . . . that thirty thousand people visited the Exhibition on the first day. (tell)

6. One engineering company was . . . . an order worth five million dollars. (give)

7. A large number of American factories have been fully . . . . (automate)

8. Several ambassadors were . . . . on the platform behind the Governor. (see)

9. How many machines were . . . . ? (exhibit)

10. How are those steel presses . . . . ? (operate)

EXERCISE B

Talking about Income Tax

Answer these questions:

PART ONE

1. Does Bill think that the House Ways and Means Committee should reduce personal income tax?

   ....

2. Why does he doubt that income tax will be reduced? Give two reasons:

   (a) ....

   (b) ....

3. Peter suggests three ways in which the Government could find money for its increased expenditures. What are they?

   (a) ....

   (b) ....

   (c) ....

4. Give (a) Bill's and (b) Peter's opinion on Federal funds for local urban renewal and poverty programs.

   (a) ....

   (b) ....

PART TWO

5. What is Peter's objection to an increased tax on luxury goods?

   ....

6.   How does Peter defend expense accounts?

. . . .

7.   Why does Peter feel that expense accounts are so important in business?

. . . .

EXERCISE C

Compare the following sentences:

(a)   The Los Angeles Dodgers have again won the World Series.
(b)   The World Series has again been won by the Los Angeles Dodgers.

Now rewrite these sentences as in (b), using the passive voice.

1.   The Americans have launched a new space-craft weighing fifty tons.

. . . .

2.   The Governor of New Jersey will open the new State Turnpike.

. . . .

. . . .

3.   Arthur Colson, the twenty-eight year old engineer from Boston, has crossed the Atlantic in a balloon.

. . . .

. . . .

4.   The National Association of Manufacturers organized the Exhibition.

. . . .

. . . .

In the remaining sentences, omit the words in italics:

5.   *The mailman* delivered your letters rather late today.

....

....

6.   *We* shall have to find more money to meet the increased expenditures.

....

....

7.   *They* certainly ought to reduce taxes.

....

8.   *The Washington Post* expects the House Ways and Means Committee to reduce income tax.

....

....

9.   *They* could find the money in a number of ways.

....

....

10. *They* could lift the wheat subsidy.

....

....

11. *They* should reduce welfare payments.

....

....